HOW TO WRITE A LOGLINE
TO INCREASE SALES

Everything an Author Should Know But Wasn't Told
About Loglines for Nonfiction and Fiction Books

Dr. Melissa Caudle

Absolute Author Publishing House, LLC

New Orleans, LA

Absolute Author
Publishing House

HOW TO WRITE A LOGLINE TO INCREASE SALES: Everything an Author Should Know But Wasn't Told About Loglines for Nonfiction and Fiction Books
Copyright ©2019 by Dr. Melissa C Caudle
All Rights Reserved

Publisher: Absolute Author Publishing House
Line Editor: Kathy Rabb Kittok
Copy Editor: Jennifer Cunningham
Proof Editor: Timothy Burke
Audible Narrator: Timothy Burke, Spoken Word Creation LLC
Cover Designer: Rebecca @Rebeccacovers
Graphics: On the Lot Productions, LLC

Library of Congress In-Publication-Data

Caudle, Melissa

HOW TO WRITE A LOGLINE TO INCREASE SALES: Everything an Author Should to Know But Wasn't Told About Loglines for Nonfiction and Fiction Books/Dr. Melissa Caudle

p. cm.

ISBN: 978-1-951028-21-3

1. Writing Resource   2. Author Resources   3. Reference

PRINTED IN THE UNITED STATES OF AMERICA

Other Reference Books By Dr. Melissa Caudle

How to Launch and Market a Book: The Six Month Countdown

How to Show and Not Tell When Writing A Novel: Everything Authors Should Know about Descriptions, Backstory, and Emotions

Fundraising for Low-Budget Films

The Reality of Reality TV: Reality Show Business Plans

The Reality of Reality TV Workbook

How to Write a Logline: Quick Guide for Screenwriters

How to Create a One Pager: Quick Guidebook for Screenwriters

150 Ways to Fund a Reality Show: Show me the Money

Just Beat it! Quick Guidebook for Screenwriters

How to Write a Synopsis: Quick Guidebook for Screenwriters

Thumbs Up! How to Nail Auditions

Novels by Dr. Melissa Caudle

The Keystroke Killer: Transcendence
A.D.A.M. The Beginning of Life
Never Stop Running
Never Stop Running Regression Journal: Documenting Your Past Lives
Secret Romances: A Forbidden Thirst for Love
Predator
Timmy's Song
A Day at the Zoo: Stephen's Big Day

Adult Coloring Books by Dr. Melissa Caudle

Abstract Faces: Adult Coloring Book Vol. 1
Abstract Faces: Adult Coloring Book Vol. 2
Abstract Faces: Adult Coloring Book Vol. 3
Abstract Faces: Adult Coloring Book Vol. 4
Abstract Faces: Adult Coloring Book Vol. 5
Cubism Faces Adult Coloring Books
Alien Faces Adult Coloring Book

TABLE OF CONTENTS

Dedication

To every author who has a dream -- dream on and write.

PREFACE

Many times, a person's path leads them in a direction of the unexpected; that is precisely what happened to me over the last two decades. I went from retiring as a central office administrator in a school district to writing and producing reality shows and films, to authoring several non-fiction books for screenwriters. Then, low and behold, I fell in love with authoring fiction and have since authored *The Keystroke Killer, Never Stop Running, A.D.A.M. The Beginning of Life*, and *Secret Romances: A Forbidden Thirst for Love*, all which came from screenplays that I wrote years before.

I must confess that it was a learning curve going from screenwriter to a novelist, but the time and effort I took to learn the craft paid off as my books consistently launch as the *#1 New Releases on Amazon*. None of this occurred as happenstance, rather long hours, and dedication to my craft. I think the good news for me was everything that I learned about writing loglines for films, scripts, and reality shows, paid off when I needed to write a logline for my first novel *The Keystroke Killer: Transcendence*. In fact, the challenging work was already complete as the novel was based on the screenplay by the same name; therefore, the characters and plot were developed. The difficulty came in making the transfer from writing descriptions that show to writing descriptions that tell and filling in the blanks that screenwriters don't have to do.

I realize that most authors don't have my history with screenplay loglines and often feel overwhelmed when asked to describe what their book is about in one or two sentences. Novelists are great at writing long descriptions, but not so much at loglines. Never fear, this book is for you. I will teach you how to write a compelling logline for your book so that you may increase your Amazon sales.

"When I don't write, I don't feel right." -- **Dr. Melissa Caudle**

ACKNOWLEDGMENTS

Writing and publishing a book is a milestone and it is something that cannot be accomplished alone. When you don't have the support of your family, it is almost impossible to achieve. Therefore, I want to acknowledge my family who supports me and encourages me to write. I can't begin to say thank you.

I also want to acknowledge my publisher, Dr. Carol Michaels, from Absolute Author Publishing House, LLC, for providing her words of wisdom, and for her friendship.

To my editor, Kathy Rabb Kittok, you know how I feel about you not only as an editor but also as my friend. Thank you for always having my back.

To my copy editor, Jennifer Cunningham, thank you for going through the first draft to clean it up before I drafted the second version.

To my audiobook narrator and final proof editor, Timothy Burke, you are awesome, and I am glad you are a part of my team.

DR. MELISSA CAUDLE

1. ALL'S FAIR IN LOVE, WAR, AND SUBJECT MATTER

"There are no dull subjects, only dull writers."

-- H.L. Menken

*H*ow to Write a Logline for Your Book to Increase Sales is considered a must-have in the publishing industry. The reason--to grab the attention of potential readers, you must be able to present your novel or book in a complete marketing package which includes an alluring sentence that is the logline. A powerful, attention-grabbing logline increases sales of your book. A logline is a narrative of the storyline in one to two sentences. Dr. Carol Michaels, CEO of Absolute Author Publishing House, says, "When authors can't narrow what their book is about in one sentence, it makes me question the rest of their manuscript. I always ask authors to submit a minimum of five different loglines because it tells me a lot about their writing style, and I learn about the book. That's how important a powerful logline is for publishers and readers. We make our decision to read the book on that one powerful sentence." Often, authors can't move from their concept that takes up hundreds of pages in their manuscript to a single sentence. When asked, "What is your book about?" authors often stammer and begin their answer by describing the character or the plot. That's not ideal as the message you're trying to deliver becomes a jumbled mess. Without an attention-getting logline, your book will be swimming with sharks in the middle of the ocean on Amazon without a chance to grab the reader's attention and possibly miss your opportunity to increase your revenue.

Some authors reading this book will already know the definition of a logline and why one is necessary, while others may think I'm speaking Greek. I'm not; rest assured. To make sure that everybody is on the same page with me, you will learn how to write your logline for your nonfiction or fiction book. Here's the best news. Not only will you learn how to write one logline but also three distinctive styles and why those three are essential for you to sell your book.

If, perchance, you have already developed your logline, please continue working through this book because you will more than likely hone it by going through the exercises. A good friend of mine always says that the best loglines are those that were thought of and rethought about time and time again.

Remember, writing is re-writing. This principle holds true for your loglines too. Keep manipulating your logline until you have the best possible one that captures the attention of the reader. This is your only objective working through this book – capture your best work you have ever written in one concise sentence.

HOW TO USE THIS BOOK

To get the most out of this book, work through one chapter at a time, and absorb the contents. Additionally, make sure to complete all the activities as they will help to perfect your logline writing ability.

Throughout the paperback and eBook, you will see two graphics that indicate the need for participation on your part and your hands-on learning activity to reinforce and develop the subject matter of the chapter. If you are listening to the audible version, you will be directed on how to proceed.

The first graphic is an activity banner. Anytime you see the activity banner or hear the words, "Activity Banner," you know there will be a creative element with an application that follows.

For you to obtain the best benefit from the information presented in this book, each activity reinforces the concept presented in the previous chapter and helps you in your journey of developing your logline.

The second graphic is for you to jot down ideas that come to your mind. I have placed one after each chapter and at the end of the book. I strongly suggest you don't wait to write any ideas down that surface as you read. If you're listening to the book, I suggest that you keep a pencil and paper handy to jot down your ideas or use your telephone to jot down your loglines as they develop. If you delay writing your ideas, you may not remember them. So, please take advantage of the learning method I provide as a professional educator with a PhD. Use the blank note pages I set aside for your notetaking and logline development. By writing your ideas in the book, you won't have to search for the piece of paper you took notes on

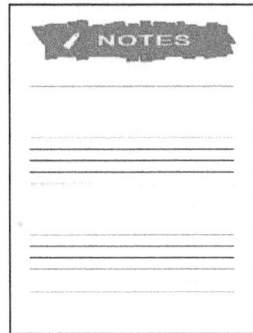

3

for future reference. How many times have you lost a piece of paper or accidentally threw one away because you didn't think it meant anything? I know I am guilty. By using the note section in this book, it prevents that and provides you with your note-taking archive. In essence, the workbook is included in this book and does not have to be purchased separately. The contents of this book won't do you any good, if you don't apply what you learn.

I know what you are thinking -- a teacher punished you for writing in your textbooks. Even when you enrolled in college, you still had a challenging time writing in them or using a highlighter. This practice isn't the case with this book. I designed the book for you to be able to write in it, mark it up, and use it to learn and grow to enhance your logline writing ability. Go ahead, start right now by getting into practice by filling in this blank. Pick up your pen or pencil and answer the following statement.

I want to create a logline for my book _____.

If you're listening to the audible version, fill in the blank, and say the title of your book aloud.

Did you fill in the blank? If not, go back and do it. Get used to writing in this book. No excuses. You bought the book, so it's yours. That is how you will be able to hone your skill to develop a compelling logline for your book. Let's begin the interactive journey.

NOTES

2. SAY IT WITH LESS

"Not that the story need be long, but it will take a long while to make it short."

-- Henry David Thoreau

The Library of Congress registers millions of books each year. According to their data for 2018, they had more than 168 million books registered in 470 languages. Wow! How do you, as an author, have your one book compete with that? This approximation does not include forthcoming manuscripts. There is an endless stream of books, and for you to make money as an author, you must be competitive. That means you must do everything within your power to put your best product forward, which includes that power-hitting logline.

WHAT IS A LOGLINE?

A logline describes your book or novel while capturing the emotional essence of it in one sentence. It is the summarization of your contents. A logline's sole purpose is to grab attention and make an individual want to know more about your book. This transfers into sales because they purchase it because they want to read it. The logline is your calling card for your novel. That's a logline in the purest form of an explanation.

Loglines for Screenplays and Television Projects

A logline does the same thing for any reality show, screenplay, or film. Designed to capture attention, it must be creative, succinct, clear, and enticing. In the golden era of Hollywood, scriptwriters wrote the loglines on the spine of the script so that producers could determine their interest. Yes, screenwriters no longer do that; however, they still must submit a logline. Think of a logline for a book as the book's DNA, which captures the character, the emotions, and the outcome. Remember, you write your logline to grab the attention of your readers. When you're asked, "What is your book about?" you don't have to manufacture something quickly because you have a logline. At all times, you should be able to answer that question when friends, family and interested parties ask it. A well-written logline will be emotionally intriguing and harnesses the interest of others encouraging them to want to know more about your book.

As an author, you must acknowledge how you will present your book to potential readers. Stand back and put yourself in the publishing world. I am co-owner of Absolute Author Publishing House, LLC (www.absoluteauthor.com), and help authors publish their books by offering editing, formatting, and marketing services. How many authors do you think contact me on any given day of the week? This includes Sundays, which by the way I usually don't work. Do you think ten? Twenty? One hundred? Two hundred? Try again. On average, I receive three hundred and fifty E-mails every day. This doesn't include the spam that bombards my account. Sorting through them takes time. My family and friends know never to send me any of the warm fuzzy stuff like cute jokes, or a funny video. I don't have time for them. My time must be spent isolating the business E-mails from my personal E-mails.

Absolute Author
Publishing House

7

Now, couple all of this with screenwriters and reality show creators sending me information about their reality show or script because I have books on how to create those as well and I own a film production company. Then, add the query letters that I receive because someone wants me to produce their film. What do you think is my first impression of these writers and creators? It's their logline.

I read the logline first, and if that grabs my interest, I'll read the treatment or synopsis. From there, if they have included the electronic press kit (EPK packet), and I like what I read, I'll look at it. You would be surprised how many authors don't know what an EPK packet is or what goes into one. If you are that person, please do your research about them for your book because you will need one. Soon, as a part of this series, I will publish a book on EPKs for authors. Therefore, please go to my blog, www.drmelmessage.com/ and subscribe to keep up-to-date on all of my new author reference books and my new novels.

Back to the E-mails. I received, within the last month, the following E-mails. They are real and have not been modified in any manner; so, please forgive the misspellings and grammatical errors. That's on them, not me. Additionally, when the original loglines appear as examples throughout this book, please remember that they have grammatical and punctuation mistakes, and I did not modify them; therefore, they are not errors in this book.

E-mail 1

> *"I have an idea for a realty book I want your company to publish. It is on me and the new life I created in New Orleans.I come here with my dog and cat and found kindnes in many people. I have always thouht I should be a character in one of your novels."*

E-mail 2

"I'll be finished with my next novel in January. I model am funny and a little crazy. It makes 4 a good time! Will you publish it for me. I read you publish books."

E-mail 3

"I am a writer. I have been working on a series of romance novels that are fiction. I would love for you to make a film from them, but first I need you to publish my novel."

E-mail 4

"I am 42 years old with 8 kids and custody of twin daughters with 7 baby mommas. I am a bouncer, bodyguard. I think my story would be a great book because I sought help with my kids. Will you be my shadow writer?"

E-mail 5

"I just moved to Los Angeles to be an actress but want to write my story. Getting an agent or manager and getting auditions is difficult. You should write my story because I am prety and I am talented."

How many do you think the examples were a joke? Just by reading them, they must be, right? Unfortunately, every E-mail was real. Again, put yourself in my shoes for a minute. Would you respond to any one of those and publish or ghostwrite their book? Heck, after reading them, would you want to read one of their books? I know I wouldn't.

It's not that any of the examples don't have potential. Truthfully, how each author wrote their logline put a negative thought about the concept into my mind. I can't get beyond the wording of each E-mail for multiple reasons:

- Lack excitement in the writing,
- Lack of a solid idea,
- Poor sentence structure,
- Misspelled words,
- Grammar mistakes,
- Punctuation errors, and
- Nothing concrete to guide development.

Are they as bad as I think? Again, I believe it is the way each statement was written and not the actual concepts.

As an experienced developmental editor and publisher, I wouldn't take a second look at any of the previous five concepts. I know intuitively if the quality of the presentation was poor, the writer likely has not developed the conceptualization; and chances are if a manuscript were attached, it was probably not well constructed or edited. What was lacking in each of the concepts was a fundamental basic -- a compelling logline to catch the attention of a publisher or reader.

Now gear up for your first hands-on activity.

ACTIVITY

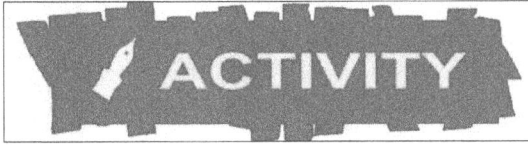

For this activity, I will reference E-mail #4. On the form below, write your answers, or if you are listening to the audible, think your answers or dictate them into the note app on your phone.

I am 42 years old with 8 kids and custody of twin daughters with 7 baby mommas. I am a bouncer, bodyguard. I think my story would be a great book. Will you be my shadow writer?

What is wrong with the way it is written?

_____

_____

Who is the book about?

_____

Do you think the concept has potential? Why or why not?

_____

_____

How can these statements be improved?

_____

_____

☻☻☻

Discussion of E-mail #4

The initial concept for the novel in E-mail #4 is about an unwed father of eight children that is a "player of sorts." That doesn't sound too bad. In fact, there is a potential inherent in the concept. However, how the author wrote the concept was grammatically incorrect and uninviting. As a publisher, I would have to initially pass or reject the novel without giving it a second thought. It's a shame because with a little work and extra thought the concept could be re-written into a presentable logline to grab mine and any other reader's attention. If fact, an entire book could be written for this concept. Couldn't you see Vin Diesel as the lead character?

That is why it is vital that you have a well-constructed logline. It could be the difference in whether the book moves up the ladder or receives a pass by a publisher, a story department developer, or if self-published, a reader. A compelling logline could make the difference whether someone cares enough to investigate the book further or purchases it. The logline serves as your calling card and a manner into the door of decision-makers -- in this case a publisher or reader. An exciting logline can open doors for you.

3. CREATING A POWERFUL LOGLINE

"My own experience is that once a story has been written, one has to cross out the beginning and the end. It is there that we authors do most of our lying."

-- Anton Chekhov

A logline format for a novel is identical for a film, a reality show or screenplay. That's the good news. The bad news is that creating a logline is not easier said than done. In fact, many authors tell me it's harder to write the logline than it is the three-hundred-page novel.

As previously stated, loglines have basic structures, and if you follow the format that I provide, you will be able to write a powerful one. It is imperative that you understand the elements of a logline before beginning your journey of writing one. The more you know, the more prepared you are to construct one.

Many times, I read sentences that authors try to pass off as loglines. The result is disastrous. Instead of grabbing my attention, the construction, or lack thereof, distracts me from the concept of the logline. It's like trying to smell a cake baking in the oven with a congested nose. Where's the enjoyment in that?

Problems in writing loglines exacerbate. If you put too much, they become cumbersome and lose the impact you desire. On the other hand, if you don't put enough, you won't make an impact at all. Where's the fine line you draw? Where do you begin developing your logline?

The answer to this question should be obvious but is overlooked by most authors. Their thinking is often flawed because they believe that if they can write a novel or book, they can write one sentence to describe it.

I'll stress the need for you to learn the basic format and structure of a logline.

List four reasons why a logline is important?

1. _____

2. _____

3. _____

4. _____

TRUE OR FALSE

_____ 1. A well-constructed logline is more likely to open the doors for your project than a poorly written one.

_____ 2. A logline is a book's calling card.

_____ 3. A logline holds the potential to grab the attention of a reader; resulting in increased sales.

Answer Key: 1. True 2. True 3. True

NOTES

4. STRUCTURE OF A LOGLINE

"Don't try to figure out what other people want to hear from you; figure out what you have to say. It's the one and only thing you have to offer."

-- Barbara Kingsolver

D o you know why NASA sends female astronauts into space? They call Houston for directions when they get lost. Now don't go and get mad at me for telling a joke about women, and please don't alert Gloria Steinem. That's not the point here in this discussion. So, I'll change the topic out of fairness.

Do you like to cook?

Do you like using your hands and assembling a bicycle or a piece of furniture out of a box?

In cooking, you follow a recipe; and unassembled items come boxed with instructions. Whether you follow a recipe or the directions that came with the item is up to you. However, instructions are there for a reason -- to guide you to perfection in the outcome.

Look at the following picture of two motocross bikers in the middle of a race. The first motorcycle barely has the lead, and the second biker is gunning the engine trying to catch him. Imagine the dust that scatters beneath the tires and the roar of the engines as they accelerate.

What do you see, or if you are listening to the book, what image comes across your mind?

The picture represents a photo that inspired a novel called *Dirt Bikers* by Charlie Wilson. It is not published yet, as I am currently editing it. When I look at the picture, I visualize the following:

- Two riders,
- Fast motion,
- Competition,
- Motocross,
- Dirt flying,
- Loud engines (Vroom),
- Crowd yelling,
- A race,
- A leader, and
- A follower.

Did you get all of that when you looked at or imagined the picture I described? Look at the picture or re-imagine it again and determine if you visualize the above elements. A powerful logline must capture the emotional essence of a concept and the elements of your book. It must accurately portray a picture so that others will see what you see.

Now let's think for a moment that I don't have a picture to show you, and if you are listening to the audible version you don't. However, I want to get you excited about the upcoming novel *Dirt Bikers* about two motocross racers. The fact is, they are brothers and during a sixth month period continued to compete until they arrived at their destination -- The National Motocross Championships. Along their journey were other racers, injuries, wrecks, sibling rivalry, and no telling what else. Which brother, if any, comes out of this victorious?

That gives you a little more information, and your challenge is to capture the novel in one sentence and not rely on a picture, that is what a compelling logline does for a book.

Here is the logline I created for *Dirt Bikers*.

Dirt Bikers – Logline

Two brothers compete and race for the national title in dirt bike motocross racing over a sixth month period and discover the true meaning of family.

What is essential to understand is that when composing a log line, there are four critical elements that need to be addressed.

- Subject,
- Verb,
- Action Description, and
- The outcome.

Here is the logline broken down for you.

1. **Subject** -- Two Brothers

2. **Verb** -- Compete

3. **Action Description** -- Race for the national title

4. **Outcome** -- Discover true meaning of family

Let's do the same thing using a different picture or a different visualization if you are listening to the audible version for the next activity banner.

Please answer the following questions as they relate to the picture. The picture is a close-up of two firemen's boots as the firemen run through knee-high flames. The wet pavement indicates that the fire crew already sprayed water in an effort to put out the fire.

What images come to you after visualizing the picture?

_____

_____

Who (subject) or what occupation (subject) is represented in this picture?

_____

_____

What are the subjects doing (action description)?

_____

_____

Where are they going because of what they are doing?

_____

_____

What do you think the outcome will be?

_____

_____

FILL IN THE BLANKS.

Martha called 911 after a _____ broke out in the apartment complex on the third floor.

Four fire trucks with thirty _____ arrived onto the scene within five minutes of Martha calling 911.

Each firefighter _____ to put out the fire to lessen the potential damage to the property and to save lives.

Because the fireman arrived quickly, _____ and her family were safe and unharmed.

Based on your answers above, identify the following components as they relate to the picture.

Who is the subject? _____

What action is evident in the picture? _____

In what process are the fireman involved?

_____

What was the outcome as a result of the fireman's response?

_____

_____

Answer Key: Answers will vary by writers.

☻☻☻☻☻

NOTES

5. ELEMENTS OF A LOGLINE

"Get it down. Take chances. It may be bad, but it's the only way you can do anything really good."

-- William Faulkner

L ike the previous application activity, compelling and well-written loglines will always have four identifiable parts which are the essential format elements that comprise them.

- **A Subject** -- indicates what or who the project or screenplay is about.

- **A Verb** -- a single word used to convey movement.

- **An Action Description** -- the process of doing or acting; what the subject does.

- **An Outcome** -- something that follows the action, the effect, or the way something turned out as a result.

Let's take a closer look at each of the four essential elements for a logline.

The Subject of the Logline

All novels are about something, somebody, or a group of people. I am not talking about your subject matter, such as a book on cooking or a biography on a serial killer. These define your topic. Instead, I am discussing who the subjects are for your book. Your subject can be a thing or topic, an individual, or a group.

Here are some examples of subjects for nonfiction and fiction books.

Table 1: Identifying Subjects

NON-FICTION BOOKS	FICTION BOOKS
Michelle Obama – *Becoming* by Michelle Obama	Bella, Jacob, Edward – *Twilight: The Twilight Saga* by Stephanie Meyer
Book Marketing – *How to Launch and Market a Book* by Dr. Melissa Caudle	A scary clown – *It* by Stephen King
Cooking Sauces – *The World Sauces Cookbook – 60 Reginal Recipes and 30 Different Pairings* by Mark C. Stevens and Susan Puckett	Zoe Morgan – *The Dark Side* by Danielle Steel
Ellen DeGeneres - *Seriously...I'm Kidding* by Ellen DeGeneres	Offred – *The Handmaid's Tale* by Margaret Atwood
Betty White - *If You Ask Me: And of Course You Won't* by Betty White	Matthew Raymond, Blaze Angela, Milo Evans, Judas Greenberg – *The Keystroke Killer* by Dr. Melissa Caudle

Goldie Hawn – *Goldie: A Lotus Grows in the Mind* by Goldie Hawn	Dr. Sandra Bradford, Jessica Parker, and General Anbar – *A.D.A.M.* by Dr. Melissa Caudle
Adult Coloring – *Cubism Faces: Adult Coloring Book* by Dr. Melissa Caudle	Jackie Hennessey – *Never Stop Running* by Dr. Melissa Caudle

You must be able to identify your subject or subjects to create the logline for your book. Complete the following activity to begin the process of developing your subject or subjects for your logline. Begin by asking, "Who is my character or who are my main characters?" or "What is my book about?"

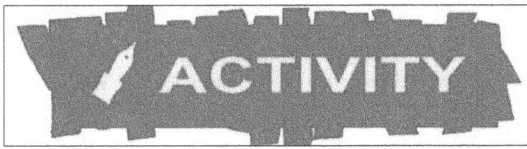

Identify the subject or subjects for your nonfiction or fiction book.

1. _____   4. _____
2. _____   5. _____
3. _____   6. _____

Narrow your list to one subject._____

Why did you choose this subject over the others?
_____
_____

Answer Key: Answers will vary by writers.

☺☺☺☺☺

NOTES

6. THE VERBS OF A LOGLINE

"A wounded deer leaps the highest."

-- Emily Dickinson

To identify a verb for your logline, ask, "What is my subject doing?" Another question to ask is, "What journey is my subject taking?" The answer to either question pinpoints the verb for your logline. Words such as *pays, jumps, rides, embarks,* and *engages* imply that something is happening.

It would be best if you used active verbs, those that a person can see another person doing, within your logline. If you are not sure whether you are using action verbs, examine each sentence and ask, "Can a person or animal or thing do this?" If your answer is, "Yes," then more than likely you are using an action verb.

To offer a clarification, a cat takes naps, a person kicks, screams, punches, blinks, swells, etc. However, can a cat "desk?" Of course not! A desk is a noun and an object. The use of an action verb will allow the reader of the logline to visualize the action. Much like our firemen in a previous activity, who "races" to put out a fire, or the motocross biker, who leans his bike into a turn.

TYPES OF VERBS

I think it is safe to say that you probably weren't expecting an English lesson today. Don't you wish you would have paid more attention in your high school English class now? Remember all those times you and your friends asked, "Why am I having to learn this; we'll never use it again?" Finally, here is your chance.

In the English language, there are three types of verbs:

- Linking verbs,
- Auxiliary verbs, and
- Action verbs.

Each verb is used differently for different purposes in a narrative or written sentence.

Linking Verbs

Linking verbs connect the subject with the rest of the sentence, usually in the form of "to be" or "could be."

Various forms of "to be" include:

- Am
- Are
- Be
- Is

- Can be
- We've
- Shall
- Being

- Has been
- Would have been
- Could have been
- Will be

Examples of the usage of linking verbs include:

- Our new star **is** a nice person.
- My book's dog **can be** a Chihuahua.
- Trip **is** a good stunt dirt bike rider.

Auxiliary Verbs

Auxiliary verbs, also known as helping verbs, assist other verbs. They usually appear in front of action verbs or linking verbs in the form of "are" or "has" or "has been."
Examples include:

- The engineers **are** meeting after the workshop today.
- The football team **has been** waiting for twenty minutes for the rain to stop.
- The car **shall** arrive in five minutes to the cafe.

Various forms of auxiliary verbs, in some instances, can also serve as linking verbs.

Examples of auxiliary verbs include:

- Can
- Could
- May
- Might
- Must
- Would
- Shall
- Should

- Will
- Had
- Has
- Have

Action Verbs

Acton verbs express or describe the behavior of a person, place, or thing. The actions may describe both physical and mental actions.

Examples of action verbs include:

- Jumps
- Joins
- Murders
- Falls
- Hunt
- Struggles

- Licks
- Races
- Weeps
- Bites
- Rescues

Examples of action verb usage include:

- Jamie **thinks** about moving to Los Angeles every day.
- Erin **honks** her horn when vehicles swerve into her path.
- Kelly **jumps** for joy when she gets a new pair of designer boots.
- The marble statue **scares** little Tommy.
- The producer **rests** on set between takes during the filming of *The Keystroke Killer*.

MAKING THE LIST

A good dictionary comes in handy to assist in the identification of creative action verbs for use in your logline. It also helps to visualize your subjects; it is what you can see because it is what they do.

There is also nothing wrong with using a Thesaurus to assist you in identifying creative verbs or creating a handy list of action verbs. In Appendix A I prepared a list of action verbs for your quick reference. When, or if, you become stuck writing your logline and need an action verb, refer to the list. It is the perfect reference tool for you.

Ideally, you won't rely solely on my list, but will continue to add to it as your skill in writing loglines develops. Use the note sheet I have provided immediately following Appendix A to add to your specialized list of action verbs. If you are an audible listener, I recommend that you use a "Notes" app on your phone and start an action verb list or when you sit at your computer, start a file.

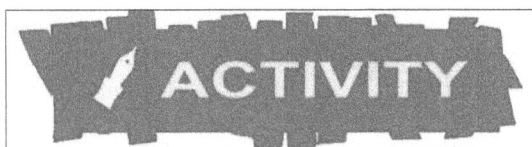

Fill in the blanks for the following loglines with an action verb from the previous list, followed by the name of the novel. Hint: these books are also films to make it easier for you to identify.

1. Just before the outbreak of War World II, Indiana Jones, _____ around the world to prevent the Nazis from stealing a significant archeological relic and learns there is more to life than just objects.

   From the novel: _____

2. In the ruins of a place once known as North America lies the nation of Panem, a shining Capitol surrounded by twelve outlying districts. The Capitol is harsh and cruel and keeps the districts in line by forcing them all to send one boy and one girl between the ages of twelve and eighteen to _____ in the annual games to the death.

   From the novel: _____

3. Edward warns Bella that she should leave him, but she refuses. A new vampire finds it a challenge to _____ Bella down for her irresistible blood. Now, the game is on, and James will not stop until she is killed.

   From the novel: _____

NOTES

7. THE ACTION DESCRIPTION

"All the words I use in my stories can be found in the dictionary—it's just a matter of arranging them into the right sentences."

-- Somerset Maugham

An author can best identify and define the action description portion of a logline by asking, "What is my subject doing?" Almost all action descriptions immediately follow the action verb within the logline. The goal is to state where the action takes your subject. In other words, the action description is a part of the action statement, but it completes the action. It is much like the famous line, "You complete me," spoken by Tom Cruise in one of my all-time favorite films *Jerry McGuire.*

Upon hearing this line, uttered by Cruise, one can't help but ask, "How does someone get completed?" Does this mean that his character wasn't complete before him announcing his incompleteness? I hope to rationalize the answer as "No." Instead, I like to think that the line adds to the character by adding specificity and detail. Unlike being dangled high above a cliff and

36

about to be let go to drop to your death, adding an action description to an already powerful verb will strengthen the picture of your book's logline. With just a few words, the logline will have more impact.

Again, consider the logline from Raiders of the Lost Ark:

> *Just before the outbreak of War World II, Indiana Jones races* ***around the world*** *to prevent the Nazis from stealing a significant archeological relic and learns there is more to life than just objects.*

The logline provides more information about the action which is "around the world." Without the inclusion of the action description, the logline doesn't carry the same connotation or weight. Here is the logline again after I removed the action description.

> *Just before the outbreak of War World II, Indiana Jones races to prevent the Nazis from stealing a relic and learns there is more to life than just objects.*

Can you determine how the two loglines differ? Which one was more powerful or interesting to you as the reader? Which way could you visualize the action or the storyline with a clearer vision?

By adding the action description following the verb in the logline, the process helps someone to visualize your subject, what your subject is engaged in performing, and leads them to a conclusion of a sort. All of this is accomplished by coupling an action verb with an action description.

8. THE OUTCOME

"Always know where you're going; life is much easier that way."

--Dr. Melissa Caudle

As with any good book or novel, it is also necessary for your subject to have a goal or a major transformation commonly known as a character arc that will be completed by the time you write, "The End." Identifying the character's transformation is how you identify the outcome for your logline. Ask, "What did, or will my subject get out this?" Also, ponder, "Did your subject undergo a transformation or did somebody else as a result of what your subject did?"

"Transmorphing"

Don't think I'm crazy, yet. I realize there isn't any such word as "Transmorphing." I made it up to make a point. When someone or something morphs, they change in configuration; a man turns into a monster, a vampire, or a zombie. Morphing involves smooth changes in shape or likeness into something different. It is the seamless transition between two images that attracts your readers. One of the first attempts at morphing was in the 1932 film *The*

Mummy and then again in 1941 in the movie *The Wolf Man*. To accomplish this effect, an actor would stand or sit in a specific position, usually marked on the floor, and the cameraman would shoot a foot of film and stop the camera. The make-up artist would run in and apply the make-up and special effects without the actor moving from their position. The camera would roll another foot and stop. This process was repeated until the desired effect was achieved. The term provided was lap dissolve. Now, with computer image processing we can "lap dissolve" much easier than in the early groundbreaking days of film. How does this apply to novel writing?

Transformation is different from morphing. Transformation implies a change of character or in nature where there is little resemblance with what once stood in structure or configuration. It is a radical change. Transformations can be physical, emotional, or refer to a new skill or relationship between others. No matter the type of transformation your subject or character goes through, the transformation aligns closely with the outcome.

Neither transformation nor morphing comprises the definition that I seek in describing the outcome for a logline. That is why I invented the new word, "Transmorphing." When the definitions of both words are combined, you gain the perspective needed to identify and write an outcome for a logline. Therefore, "Transmorphing" is defined as the smooth and transitional process of a character that reflects a change of character, or nature into a newly developed entity. A new person is born within the old physical body -- the outcome, or endgame a character becomes.

Once you have identified the outcome, it is easier for you to include it in your logline. For example, in the logline for *Raiders of the Lost Ark*, Indiana Jones learns there is more to life than acquiring objects.

> *Just before the outbreak of War World II, Indiana Jones races around the world to prevent the Nazis from stealing a significant archeological relic **and learns there is more to life than just acquiring objects**.*

Consider the following logline from *Hoops: Life off the Court* by David Reiner.

*A group of college basketball players engages in life off the court as they develop team dynamics and **learn what it takes to be champions**.*

The boys, after a series of trials and errors, come away with new skills and realize the importance of working as a team to win the championship.

In review, without exception, a compelling logline always contains four essential elements.

1. **A Subject** -- indicates what or who the project is about.

2. **A Verb** -- a single word used to convey movement.

3. **An Action Description** -- the process of doing or acting; what the subject does.

4. **An Outcome** -- something that follows the action, the effect, or the way something turned out as a result.

VARY YOUR LOGLINE

To vary a logline, the order of each element doesn't matter. Often, by adjusting an element's placement in the sentence, a logline gains excitement and is more enticing to the reader.

For example, the logline for *Dirt Bikers* can easily be re-ordered and still maintain the clarity of the novel.

Original Logline for *Dirt Bikers*

Two brothers compete and race for the national title in dirt bike racing over a sixth month period and discover the true meaning of family.

The above logline is in the following order.

- **A Subject** -- Two brothers
- **A Verb** -- compete
- **An action** -- race for the national title in dirt bike racing
    - **An Outcome** -- discover the true meaning of family

When I change the order of the four elements of the logline, the logline meaning doesn't change. Consider the next examples and notice the placement order of the four elements.

Modified Loglines for *Dirt Bikers*

Example 1

The national dirt bike racing title is on the line as two brothers vie for the title and discover the true meaning of family.

This logline is in the following order: Action, subject, verb, and outcome.

Example 2

Two brothers learn the true meaning of family as they vie for the national dirt bike racing title.

This logline is in the following order: Subject, outcome, verb, action.

Example 3

During a dirt bike championship rally, two brothers learn the value of family as they compete for the national title.

This logline is in the following order: Action, subject, outcome, and verb.

Did you notice how the four elements were re-arranged? The order of the elements didn't change the meaning of the logline. In essence, they are doppelgangers and could be used interchangeably to vary press releases, blog posts, book trailer descriptions and more.

Now consider these loglines.

Example 1

Hoops: Life off the Court

A group of college basketball players engage in life off the court as they develop team dynamics.

Example 2

Never Stop Running - by Dr. Melissa Caudle

A young woman undergoes hypnosis and realizes the impact her past life has on her current relationships.

Example 3

A.D.A.M. - by Dr. Melissa Caudle

The Beginning of New Life

NASA scientist, Dr. Sandra Bradford, discovers a new life form and becomes the target of a government assassination plot only to outsmart them.

In each the above loglines, the four different elements – subject, verb, action, and outcome are present.

Let's take a closer look at the loglines.

Example 1

Hoops: Life off the Court

A group of college basketball players engage in life off the court as they develop team dynamics.

- **Subject** -- A group of six college basketball players with nothing in common
- **Verb** -- engage
- **Action Description** -- in life off the court

43

- **Outcome** -- as they develop team dynamics

Example 2

A.D.A.M. - **by Dr. Melissa Caudle**

NASA scientist, Dr. Sandra Bradford, discovers a new morphing life form and becomes the target of a government assassination plot only to outsmart them.

- **Subject** -- NASA scientist, Dr. Sandra Bradford
- **Verb** -- discovers a new morphing life form beneath Mono Lake and
- **Action Description** -- becomes the target of a government assassination plot
- **Outcome** -- only to outsmart them.

Do you recognize the four elements in each logline? Clearly, loglines are complex. However, once you figure out the formula, writing them becomes straightforward.

The more you practice dissecting loglines, the better logline writer you become. Please keep in mind that practicing something in itself isn't enough. You can practice until you are blue in the face, but if what you are practicing is wrong, the results won't be right. Therefore, perfect practice is the key.

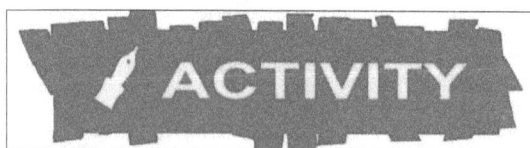

ACTIVITY

Identify the four elements in the following logline as they relate to the still photo and the novel *The Triple Crown Jockey* (not a real book). If you are listening to the audible version,

the picture is that of five jockeys on their horses jostling for position as they come around a curve during a horse race.

Twelve apprentice jockeys compete for the right to become the jockey for the racehorse Triple Crown.

1. **Subject -** _____

2. **Verb -** _____

3. **Action Description -** _____

4. **Outcome -** _____

ANSWER KEY –*1. Twelve apprentice jockeys 2. Compete 3. For the right ride Triple Crown 4. Winner and gets to race the horse Triple Crown.*

☻☻☻☻☻

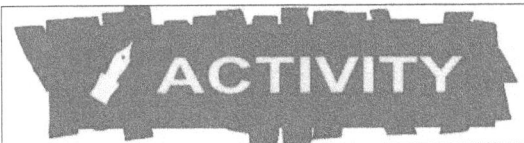

Identify the four elements to the logline below from *The Baker Girls: Sealed with a Kiss. (Not a real novel)*

45

(1_____) Five retail salesgirls in a mall (2_____)
embark (3_____) on life after work (4_____)
as they develop friendships within the circle.

Consider the next logline and answer the following questions about *Never Stop Running* by Dr. Melissa Caudle

A young woman undergoes hypnosis recounting her past lives and realizes the impact her deaths have on her current relationships.

1. What is the subject of the above logline?
_____

2. What is the verb of the above logline?
_____

3. What is the action of the above logline_____

4. What is the outcome of the above logline?_____

NOTES

9. ENHANCING A LOGLINE

"It's none of their business that you have to learn to write. Let them think you were born that way."

-- Ernest Hemingway

In some ways, reading a well-written logline is like watching a good movie. Now that you now have a basic understanding of loglines, and the four elements a compelling logline requires, it's time to start enhancing them to make them more powerful. To make certain that your logline grabs the attention of the reader, there are specific enhancement techniques used by authors.

These include adding:

- A time frame,
- The ethnicity of the subject,
- The age of the subject or character,
- Names of the protagonist and antagonist,
- Occupation of the protagonist,
- Conflict or crisis,

- Adjectives to any of the four elements,
- Character traits to the subject, and
- The emotional state of the subject.

Timeframe Enhancement

To enhance loglines, modify the timeframe. Here is the logline from the *Dirt Bikers*.

> *During a period of six months, two brothers vie for the national dirt bike racing title they have trained for since they were children.*

From this logline, we can determine the entire process for the dirt bike race preparation will take six months. We also know that the brothers have been riding dirt bikes since they were children. This is new information, but it does not modify the original context of the logline. It simply provides additional information about the novel we didn't know before.

Adding Age to the Logline

When an author provides the age of the protagonist, it helps to guide the reader and provides a better understanding of the motive behind him or her. Consider the following logline from *Never Stop Running*.

> *A young woman undergoes hypnosis recounting past lives and realizes the impact her past lives have on her current relationships.*

The logline for *Never Stop Running* tells the reader, in one sentence, the concept of the novel -- a woman undergoing hypnosis. Our subject, or in this case, our protagonist is a young woman. Notice I didn't include the young woman's name or her age. Does that make you wonder how young is young?

To remove any doubt of the age of the character, some authors choose to include the age of the character in the logline. When doing so, there are two ways to add that information for the most impact.

1. In the beginning of the logline, or

2. After the subject's name or title.

Consider the following examples.

Age Enhancement Logline 1 – Beginning of the Logline

*A **thirty-two-year-old** woman undergoes hypnosis recounting past lives and realizes the impact her past lives have on her current marriage.*

Age Enhancement Logline 2 – After the Subject's Name or Title

*A young woman, **age thirty-two**, undergoes hypnosis recounts past lives and realizes the impact her past lives have on her current relationships.*

By adding her age to the logline, we get a better idea of where the main character is in her professional life as well as the age range of the character. That factor alone informs any reader that the protagonist is in her thirties and not considered a young college student or a woman experiencing a mid-life crisis.

Adding a Character's Name to a Logline

Many authors also opt to include the name of the protagonist, antagonist, or other characters to enhance a logline. Ethnic names in nature are often revealing in loglines. For instance, the name

Rebecca Goldstein could provide a clue. What ethnic group do you think she or what religious affiliation do you believe she may associate and claim as her own?

Often, a name ending in "Stein" is reflective of the Jewish community. However, don't let a name fool you. She could have married and changed her last name. That is why a writer offers clarity in the logline with a specific name if it is important to that character. For example, in the following logline from my next novel *Protected*, it is important that the audience knows that the protagonist comes from a wealthy Jewish family.

Name Enhancement Logline 1

A wealthy Jewish girl tries to fit into her new school after her dad's imprisonment for bank fraud and is forced into the witness protection program with a new family.

In this example, it is important that we know that our main character is Jewish and having to adjust to a different lifestyle and religion. Her world turns upside down; she can no longer practice anything associated with her Jewish culture, and all her fancy designer clothes are traded for the local "Super Store" style.

If you know anything about the United States' *Witness Protection Program,* when you enter it, you must leave everything and everyone you knew behind. You can't have any contact with former friends or family, you cannot work in the same occupation that you once did, you can't hold the same type of job, and you can't practice the same religion. In essence, you become a new you. Once in witness protection, you are "Transmorphed." This back-story drives the need to identify an ethnic surname in the logline for the novel *Protected*.

Another example is from a short novella I wrote called *Tommy's Song.* Without knowing anything about this story, you can determine that the main character is Tommy and the storyline must have to do with some sort of a song, correct? This is another example of when it is important to include the name of the protagonist into a logline. Think about the following example.

Name Enhancement Logline 2

Tommy, a high school senior football star, struggles to record an original song to get into a prestigious music college after a career-ending injury.

When it isn't important to identify a specific ethnic group with a name, you can choose any name to your liking. To demonstrate this concept, notice that in the name enhancement for *Never Stop Running,* it does not state the character's name or the hypnotist's name. Now consider the following enhanced version where first and last names were added for both the protagonist and the antagonist.

Name Enhancement Logline 3

Jackie Hennessey, age thirty-two, undergoes hypnosis by Dr. Grayson, only to recount past lives; which complicates her relationship with David, her husband of eight years

By adding the name of the characters, we learn who the protagonist and antagonist are as well as a supporting character. They somehow transfer into people we can identify as real. It is like meeting a person for the first time. When you see them again, would you rather say, "Hey you!" or call them by name and say, "Hello, Jackie?" I find it a lot more comfortable calling someone by name rather than by a generic phrase like, "I met a young woman." The more friendly version is, "I met Jackie, an incredible young woman." Readers of loglines are no different, and sometimes they long for more information without it being thrown into their face.

For example, suppose I change the name of Jackie Hennessey to Aditi Bhaskara and Dr. Grayson to Dr. Marie Laveau. Would these name changes have any impact on your interpretation of the logline for *Never Stop Running*? Let's look at the name enhancement logline 3 modified to reflect the aforementioned name changes.

Name Enhancement Logline 4

*Diti Bhaskara, age 32, undergoes hypnosis by **Dr. Maire Laveau,** only to recount past lives; which complicates her current relationship with David, her spouse.*

What significance do the names represent now, and how do they affect the logline?

First, let's examine the name Aditi Bhaskara. What culture do you associate the surname of Bhaskara? Is it Greek? African American? German? None of those make any sense. Bhaskara is a name that originates from the country of India. Most people from India practice a certain religion and believe in reincarnation and past lives. Therefore, if my thirty-two-year-old woman was born in India and her family migrated to America when she was a child, it wouldn't be too much of a stretch for her to seek her past life through hypnosis. The name Jackie Hennessey doesn't reflect a religious belief, so the interpretation as to what she believes about the concept of past life experiences and reincarnation is left wide open. By her name alone, we don't know if she has a problem accepting the concept of past life experiences or whether she believes in reincarnation. We only know her relationship with David, her husband, is compromised and becomes more complicated as her past lives emerge through the hypnosis sessions.

The name of the hypnotist tells us a lot too. First, Dr. Grayson could be any race, a man or a woman, and any age. The surname itself is Welsh having its origin in Scotland. This still doesn't offer much for us to go on. There's not much more we can deduce from the name. It is open to interpretation.

Let's say, for argument sake, I changed Dr. Grayson's name to Dr. Maire Laveau. First, this narrows the character to a woman's name. The name also has a certain connotation associated in a New Orleans historical aspect. In the history and culture of New Orleans, Marie Laveau is a central figure associated with Voodoo. The daughter of a White planter and a Black slave in 1782, she was born a free woman. She is responsible for having had profound influence over a multiracial following during the 1870s.

Given this information, a hypnotist by the name of Dr. Maire Laveau might lead us to believe that she practiced more than just hypnotism and might add a little drama to the mix which leads us to our next enhancement-- adding an occupation.

Occupation Enhancement

Adding your character's occupation can enhance your logline and provide specificity. Would the result of the hypnosis session be different for Jackie because of the occupation of either Dr. Laveau or Dr. Grayson? Think about the two following loglines for *Never Stop Running* and the impact occupation has after I enhanced them with the occupation of one character.

Example for Dr. Laveau

> *Jackie Hennessey, age thirty-two, undergoes hypnosis by **Dr. Maire Laveau,** a voodoo priestess, only to recount past lives; which complicates her current relationship with David, her spouse.*

Example for Dr. Grayson

> *Jackie Hennessey, age thirty-two, undergoes hypnosis by **Dr. Grayson,** Mount Sanai Head of Psychological Department of Research, only to recount past lives; which complicates her current relationship with David, her spouse.*

What have you learned? First is the occupation of the hypnotherapist. Watch out! Which one is more acceptable to you?

There is no right or wrong answer here. What is essential is for the reader to make an emotional connection. Some readers will love the fact that Jackie sought help from a voodoo priestess while others may cringe and believe she would best be served by a medical practitioner like Dr. Grayson. The bottom line for me was that I chose Dr. Grayson as a licensed professional, which also reflected the connotation and tone of the storyline.

For my novel *A.D.A.M.*, it is important to know that the main character, Dr. Sandra Bradford, is employed by NASA and that she is a scientist. Once again, here is the logline from *A.D.A.M.*

Example 1

NASA scientist, Dr. Sandra Bradford, discovers a new morphing life form and becomes the target of a government assassination only to outsmart them.

Her profession explains how she came by the opportunity to discover a new life form. It wouldn't make sense if she was a high school English teacher. Therefore, it is important to include her occupation.

Adding a Location to Your Logline

Adding the location in which the novel takes place can enhance a logline. For instance, using my novel, Never *Stop Running*, and the location, would it make a difference if I informed you that the book was set in New Orleans? What if the office of Dr. Grayson, the hypnotherapist, is in the original house that Marie Leveau lived while in New Orleans and the character's name changed to Dr. Mark Leveau? How important is it to identify the location in that case? Sometimes it is important for readers to know the location in which your novel takes place. By doing so, it not only can create a certain vibe for your book; but it can also provide details on where the characters live and a feeling for their surroundings.

As an author, you must determine if it is necessary at all. There are occasions where you should include it. For example, consider a memoir by one of the stars of *The Real Housewives of Atlanta*. We know that this show took place in Atlanta and every time there is a spin-off, the name changes to reflect it. The location is especially important to include in a logline for situations such as this.

Now, look at the following loglines for *Big Night* and *Bridges of Madison County*.

Example 1 - *Big Night* by Stanley Tucci

Two brothers struggling to keep their 1950s New Jersey Italian restaurant from foreclosing invite Louis Prima and his band to take part in an extravagant dinner party.

Example 2 – *Bridges of Madison County* by Clint Eastwood

Stuck in her humdrum daily life, an Iowa housewife must choose between the needs of her family and true romance.

Both loglines provide the location. For *Big Night*, it is important for readers to know that the restaurant is in New Jersey, which brings specific images to the reader's mind as well as puts certain character traits for the subject in place. As for *Bridges of Madison County*, having it set in Iowa provides a visual image of farm life or small-town life. The location explains the main character wanting to break from her daily routine.

Now let's go back to the logline from *Never Stop Running*. We have been developing with enhancements, added a location to it, and another element we didn't know before.

Jackie Hennessey, 32, from New Orleans undergoes hypnosis by Dr. Grayson, only to recount past lives which complicate her relationship with David, her husband.

What do you know about Jackie now? What images come to your mind with your knowledge that she is from New Orleans and not from Miami Beach? You need to ask, "Does adding the location enhance the logline, detract from it, or does it make any difference?" If adding the location enhances your logline, then by all means include it. However, if adding a location detracts, or it doesn't make any difference, then don't include it.

Adding a Crisis or Turmoil the Subject Faces to the Logline

Another technique to enhance a logline is to include a crisis or turmoil to your protagonist's situation, which propels the plot of your novel resulting in a more significant impact. Consider this enhanced logline from *Never Stop Running.*

> *Jackie Hennessey, age thirty-two, **after a severe accident results in amnesia,** undergoes regression hypnosis by Dr. Grayson only to recount past lives which complicate her relationship with David, her spouse.*

By enhancing the logline for *Never Stop Running* with a crisis, the reader obtains a clear understanding as to why the subject undergoes hypnosis, and the logline has an attention-grabbing detail that it didn't have before. Undergoing regression hypnosis doesn't have anything to do with Jackie's religious beliefs or whether she believes in reincarnation. We now know that she had a serious accident which caused amnesia.

Adding a Character Trait to the Logline

To enhance a logline further, use adjectives to describe a character's traits. Character traits come in all forms and behaviors to make a character more interesting and diverse. Sample character traits include emotions, whereas others describe behaviors. The goal of adding an adjective that describes the character or subject is to tell us something about him or her.

Is the character fearless? Dishonest? Selfish? Ambitious? There are numerous character traits from which to choose. Notice how the logline for *Never Stop Running* changes in tone after I enhanced it.

> *Jackie Hennessey, **a perfectionist**, undergoes hypnosis by Dr. Grayson, after a serious accident results in amnesia, only to recount **murderous** past lives; which complicate her relationship with her spouse, David.*

Once the character trait of a "perfectionist" was added to the logline, we know a lot more about Jackie. We know that before the accident she was a perfectionist. Any perfectionist would have a challenging time not only admitting a character flaw but also having to cope with amnesia. When adding "murderous" as an adjective to her reincarnated past lives, we gain knowledge that her past lives are not the white picket *Leave It to Beaver* type; but more like the shower scene in Alfred Hitchcock's *Psycho*.

By enhancing your logline with character traits, they also add a dramatic effect and make it more exciting and intriguing. In Appendix B, I have included a list of character traits that you can use when describing your character and subjects in your logline.

Adding an Emotional State to the Logline

Often, if you include the emotional state that a character is in, it provides an element of enhancement. All great novels have the main subject go through an emotional journey. So, why not include it in your logline?

Now, consider this logline from *Never Stop Running*.

> *Jackie Hennessey, a **distraught** perfectionist, undergoes hypnosis to recover her memories only to find herself more **confused** by her **emotional journey** as past lives emerge and complicate her relationship with her husband.*

The enhancement of the emotional state of Jackie takes us on a complete journey in this logline. We not only can feel that she is distraught, but she is distraught for several reasons -- she lost her memory, she is confused, she is no longer perfect, she has complications with her husband, and so forth. A great deal emerges about Jackie's character in just a few words when we add her emotional journey to the mix.

Adding a Basic Desire to the Logline

You can also zero in on a basic desire your character has to enhance a logline that will also grab the attention of the reader. These enhancements always add flair and spice.

The impact of the logline for *Never Stop Running* changes to reveal something about our main character when a basic desire is added.

> *Jackie Hennessey*, a distraught amnesia accident victim, ***who wants her life to return to normal***, *undergoes hypnosis to recover her memories only to find herself more confused by her emotional journey as past lives emerge impacting her relationship with her family.*

As we have developed this logline, this is the first time we get a feeling that Jackie isn't happy with things in her life after the accident and wants something that is driving her to seek hypnosis. Her only desire is to have her upside-down life return to normal. Does this mean she is willing to try hypnosis?

Making Sense of Enhancements in Loglines

Which of these loglines for *Never Stop Running* do you like?

Logline 1

A Young woman undergoes hypnosis and recounts past lives realizing the impact her past deaths have on her current relationships.

Logline 2

Jackie Hennessey, a perfectionist, undergoes hypnosis by Dr. Grayson, after a serious accident results in amnesia, only to recount murderous past lives which complicate her relationships.

Logline 3

Jackie Hennessey, a distraught accident victim, who wants her life to return to normal, undergoes hypnosis to recover her memories only to find herself more confused by her emotional journey as past lives emerge impacting her relationship with her family.

Did you like it plain and simple like the logline in Example 1, or did you find one of the enhanced versions more suitable to your liking in Examples 2 and 3?

Do you have any clue as to why you like one over the other?

Which logline would more likely draw you to read *Never Stop Running*?

These are some of the many questions to address when you develop your book's logline. This is how you begin to hone and develop a logline that is compelling.

Start with a basic concept or outline for your logline. Work with it, manipulate it, and use one or more of the enhancements we've discussed. Don't overwork your logline by using every enhancement technique, or it is likely to get crazy. Your goal is to define your novel in terms that will be attention-grabbing for the reader. Remember, your goal in using a well-developed logline is to increase sales, and to do that you have to grab a reader's attention. Variety is going to be the key to writing your logline. The point is to have a logline that sounds great and is easy for you to recite.

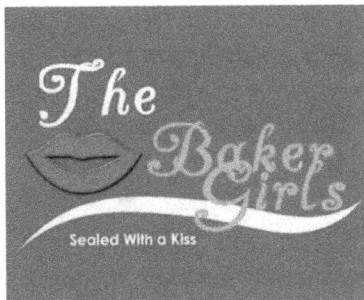

The following loglines are variations for *The Baker Girls: Sealed with a Kiss*. This time I restructured each one to emphasize how the four elements can be re-arranged for impact. In the first example, I start with the outcome followed by the subject, verb, and action, and then I reformat the logline and begin with the action. The last one I start with the subject again but add a conflict. Notice that I often added words to enhance a logline. That is how loglines start developing. Ultimately, you end up with one logline that becomes your favorite.

The Baker Girls: Sealed with a Kiss – by Dr. Melissa Caudle

Example 1

As they develop friendships within their circle, five retail salesgirls at a Baker's store in a mall embark on life after work.

Example 2

Life after work for five retail girls proves to be more than friendship as each one relies on the others to make it through their day.

Example 3

Five friends who work together at a local store develop friendships; which proves more than they can handle on weekends.

Example 4

As they develop friendships within their circle, five gorgeous retail sales girls at a Baker's store in an urban mall embark on New Orleans's party life after work in the famous French Quarter.

Example 5

Party Life on Bourbon Street after work for five Playmate-type retail girls proves to be more than friendship as each one relies on the others to make it through personal crises of love, lust, and lies.

Example 6

Five beauty queens, who work together at a rural shoe store in Mississippi, develop lasting friendships as they undergo personal changes while enduring hardships in their lives.

Did you recognize the different enhancements used in these examples? Did any of them affect the way you interpret the tone of the novel? Could you easily identify the four structural elements that compelling loglines have?

Also, remember the more you manipulate your logline by adding and taking enhancements away, the more effective your logline becomes. It is a matter of putting together the right ingredients to formulate it exactly how you like it, while ultimately grabbing the attention of readers. That is the power of compelling loglines verses poorly written and ill-fated ones. Empower yourself when writing your loglines by practicing writing them. The key is not only writing a logline but also to perfect it.

NOTES

_____
_____
_____
_____
_____
_____
_____
_____
_____
_____
_____
_____
_____
_____
_____
_____
_____
_____
_____
_____
_____
_____
_____
_____
_____
_____
_____
_____

10. TWO - THREE SENTENCE LOGLINES

"You learn by writing short stories. Keep authoring short stories. The money's in novels, but writing short stories keeps your writing lean and pointed."

-- **Larry Niven**

Another way to bring a dramatic flair to your logline is to make your logline more than one sentence and use several of the enhancing features. For example, let's examine the original logline for my novel *A.D.A.M.*

NASA scientist, Dr. Sandra Bradford, discovers a new morphing life form and becomes the target of a government assassination plot only to outsmart them.

By reading the logline, you know that a NASA scientist becomes a target of a government conspiracy after she discovers a new life form. Umm? If I modify the logline according to my enhancement suggestions, first by adding a character trait or

64

adjective, then include a crisis, add how she copes with it, and then make it three sentences instead of one, the logline dramatically changes. Let's look at it now.

> *NASA lead **astrobiological physicist**, Dr. Sandra Bradford **researches a cure** for the **disease that killed her infant son** and discovers a new morphing life form. She tries to keep his existence a secret from the government. When she becomes the target of a government conspiracy, her secret is revealed.*

By breaking the logline to *A.D.A.M.* into three sentences and adding the emotional state, a crisis, an adjective to the profession, and how the subject responds, do you see how the logline has been enhanced? The novel hasn't changed. The only thing that changed was the logline structure.

First, we now know that Dr. Sandra Bradford is a lead astrobiological physicist at NASA and is grieving for the loss of her son that died from some incurable disease. We also discover that while researching a cure she finds a new life form that morphs. The irony is she doesn't want anyone to know, but because she has become a target of a government cover-up, she must tell somebody. We get all that information by adding a few keywords to the original logline. In essence, the three sentences define the three acts to the plot of the novel.

If you find the three-sentence logline structure cumbersome, try writing a two-sentence one. An example for *A.D.A.M.* follows.

> *After discovering a new life form, a NASA research scientist, becomes the target of a government assassination plot and feels compelled to reveal her secret to the public.*

Which one would make you want to read the novel? My philosophy is if I can get my concept out in one sentence, that is the way to do it.

Now let's look at the loglines from *The Baker Girls: Sealed with a Kiss*. I've already rewritten them to include several enhancements.

Example 1 – Original Logline

As they develop friendships within their circle, five retail sales girls at a Baker's store in a mall embark on life after work.

Example 2 – Enhanced Logline

Mandy, Kelly, Jamie, Veronica, and Alyson develop friendships that prove more than they can handle weekends in the party capital of America – New Orleans. Lessons are learned, loves are lost, and lies told as drama unfolds for these party divas.

Now you are familiar with different loglines for several of my novels. You have read them in simple versions as well as enhanced.

Do you have a favorite one or style for any of them? If so, you could be developing a pattern of how you like loglines to read and that can tell you a lot about the type of loglines you will create. You may like loglines that start with action words or those that begin with the subject. Three-sentence or two-sentence loglines might read better to you. In the end, you will develop your own style and pattern.

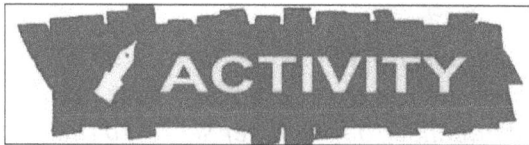

Rewrite the following loglines starting with either the outcome or the action first.

Never Stop Running **by Dr. Melissa Caudle**

A young woman who undergoes hypnosis recounts her past lives and realizes the impact her past deaths have on her current life.

_____

_____

_____

_____

_____

A.D.A.M. by Dr. Melissa Caudle

NASA scientist Dr. Sandra Bradford discovers a new morphing life form and becomes the target of a government conspiracy only to outsmart them and reveal her finding to the public.

_____

_____

_____

_____

Hoops: *Life off the Court* by Dr. Melissa Caudle

A group of college basketball players engage in life off the court as they develop team dynamics.

_____

_____

_____

_____

_____

Answer Key: Answer will vary.

☺☺☺☺☺

ACTIVITY

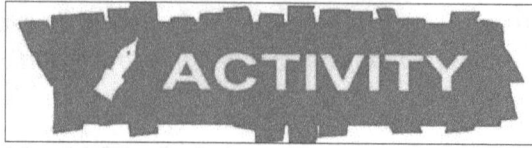

Rewrite the following logline for my novel *Secret Romances: A Forbidden Thirst for Love* four different ways and include a different enhancement technique you learned in this chapter.

When Angela becomes the new CEO of her father's magazine, she faces obstacles as she defies him with her new lover who is not in her social status.

Logline 1

_____
_____
_____
_____

Logline 2

_____
_____
_____
_____

Logline 3

_____
_____
_____
_____

Logline 4

_____
_____
_____
_____

NOTES

20

11. THE DO'S AND DON'TS OF LOGLINES

"It is perfectly okay to write garbage—as long as you edit brilliantly."

-- C. J. Cherryh

Authors often ask me, "What are the Do's and Don'ts when writing a logline?" So, I have listed them for you.

Do...

> ➤ Take time to develop your logline but develop it first before your concept.
> ➤ Hone and polish your logline throughout the writing phase.
> ➤ Up to the last moment, consider your logline a work in progress.
> ➤ Write at least twelve different loglines for your novel. Manipulate them in a different arrangement using different verbs and enhancements. One of them you will fall in love with and use.
> ➤ Make sure that your logline sounds fantastic to the reader.

➤ Make sure your logline is easy to remember and can be recited instantly upon request.

➤ Ask your friends and relatives which loglines you created sticks with them.

➤ Be open to suggestions from others if they come up with one.

➤ Keep your logline to one sentence. Only use the two or three sentence loglines for marketing purposes.

➤ Practice writing loglines by changing the order of the four elements. They don't always have to appear in the same order.

➤ Feel free to add what type of genre your book falls into. This can add some spice to your logline.

➤ Focus on the uniqueness of your novel.

➤ Be brief.

Don't...

➤ Don't include the entire concept of your novel by telling every detail. You don't need to write a spoiler alert.

➤ Never use analogies such as, "It's Ozzy Osbourne meets Donald Trump." Analogies are amateur.

➤ Never use clichés.

➤ Never claim, or even come close to claiming, that your novel is absolutely the best on the market unless you have received a best-seller award from the *New York Times*, *USA Today* or your book has been recommended by Oprah for her book club.

➤ Don't complicate your logline by using words nobody understands but you. Keep them simple but enticing.

➤ Never go over more than three sentences.

LOGLINE WORKSHOP

By now, you should be familiar with logline structure and enhancement features. I want to take you back to the beginning of this book. Do you remember when I first brought up the poorly written loglines that I received in emails? They included misspellings, poor style and format, and many unappealing elements. Let's apply what we have learned to make them pop and grab attention.

Example 1 – Dad with Eight Children

Original Concept Received

> *"I am 42 years old with 8 kids and custody of twin daughters with 7 baby mommas. I am a bouncer, bodyguard. I think my story would be a great book because I sought help with my kids. Will you be my shadow writer?"*

How to Identify the Subject

Ask: Who is this novel about?

In the above poorly written logline, I first must identify the subject for the project by asking, "Who is this story about?" It is about the dad. That is clear. So, I extracted the information and identified the subject.

Subject Answer

> Dad, who is a bouncer, bodyguard and has eight children by different mothers.

How to Identify the Action Verb

Ask: What is the action verb that best describes the action?

Identifying the action verb is a little trickier because it is not specifically stated in the logline for our playboy dad. You must infer what the storyline in this novel will concern. This is when the list of action verbs in Appendix A comes in handy. When an obvious action verb doesn't come to me, I'll refer to the list. While I am searching the list, I ask myself, "What is the subject trying to do?" Before I know it, I can isolate an action verb that fits perfectly.

My search through the action list revealed the action verb "Juggles." I immediately knew that was the verb I wanted to use. The dad is juggling his time between his job as a bouncer and bodyguard, his children, and having to deal with seven different mothers to his children. I had my action verb.

I transferred the word juggling into the bland action verb area.

A dad juggles between his jobs as a bouncer and bodyguard and maneuvers between the seven mothers of his eight children.

How to Identify the Action

Ask: What is the subject doing?

To determine the action, after the verb, I must identify what the subject is doing. I already identified the action verb "Juggling," so I asked, "What is he juggling?" It is obvious to me, by in the concept, that he is juggling everything in his life. I now am almost complete with my logline.

A dad juggles between his jobs as a bouncer and bodyguard as he balances his life between the seven mothers of his eight children.

How to Identify the Outcome

Ask: What does the Subject learn or what changes does my subject make?

The only thing left is to figure out what the outcome is for the logline. Again, it is not clearly defined, but inferred in the original statement.

For any outcome, the subject will either deal with it or be overwhelmed. Likewise, the subject will have to come to terms with the circumstances presented daily. Changes often occur within the subject. To find the outcome, I asked, "What did the subject learn?" I also asked, "How did the subject change?"

The outcome -- he seeks help to cope and deal with his life or turns to his friends for support, etc. You might be thinking that there wasn't anything stated in the original concept about our dad needing help from his friends or needing support. You are wrong, it simply wasn't clear. That was one of the major flaws in the original logline. Therefore, as an author, you must define the outcome for your character and include it in the logline. In this case, I used my judgment. I know that when people are in demanding situations, they seek support. I would make sure that my main character, in this case, the dad, sought help from a family therapist or life coach.

Since I have all of the four elements identified, it is a matter of transferring the information and writing the logline.

A forty-two-year-old dad juggles his career as a bouncer and a bodyguard, his eight children and seven mothers by seeking the advice a life coach.

I had a simple logline that I could manipulate and enhance. I began by strengthening the simple logline with adjectives, defined his careers, gave him a name, and added a conflict element by including dealing with the seven mothers of his children.

Enhancement 1

John, a forty-two-year-old playboy, with eight kids from seven different mothers, including twin daughters, juggles his career as a celebrity bodyguard and his love life as he seeks help from a life coach to change his ways.

Again, this logline can be further developed and enhanced in a variety of ways. For example, here is a different logline.

Enhancement 2

John, a forty-two-year-old playboy with eight kids from seven different mothers, juggles his career and family life. When his life falls apart, he seeks help from a life coach to change his ways and learns that being a dad is more than just being a sperm donor.

Notice how I wrote the revised loglines. I didn't use every word or sentence that the original contained. I did use the concept and kept the same premise as presented to me. To narrow it and make it more appealing, I followed the same rules and techniques I presented throughout this book. I also added the outcome. In other words, I practiced what I preached.

Reflect on the loglines for just a minute. What would you title this novel? A good title might be *The Playboy Dad* or *Dad Wars.* The only reason I bring this up is to point out that often the title of the project impacts the way we interpret a logline. Keep this in mind as you put a title to your novel. Ask, "Does the logline reflect the type of genre for my novel?"

Now let's do the same thing with another poorly written example from the wannabe actress who moved to Los Angeles.

Example 2 - Original Concept (semi-edited for spelling and grammar)

"I just moved to Los Angeles to be an actress but want to write my story. Getting an agent or manager and getting auditions is difficult. You should write my story because I am pretty, and I am talented."

Ask: Who is this novel about?

Subject - Young "wannabe" actress

Ask: What is the action verb that best describes the action?

Verb – struggles

Ask: What is the subject doing?

Action – trying to get an agent or manager, and become an actress in Los Angeles

Ask: What does the subject learn, or what changes does the subject make?

Outcome – unknown; will have to be added.

New Logline

A wannabe actor seeks fame and fortune in Hollywood overcoming the obstacles of finding an agent, which changes the way she perceives herself.

Notice how the information was abstracted, or if it wasn't clear, I added it. For example, the outcome wasn't clearly stated. I have found that for first-time logline writers determining the outcome is the most difficult part and requires a lot of brainstorming. With practice, you will become good at it.

A good title for this novel would be *Seeking Fame and Fortune,* or *The Hollywood Seeker.* Again, notice how a name change for the same novel has an impact on how you view it.

FINAL LOGLINES

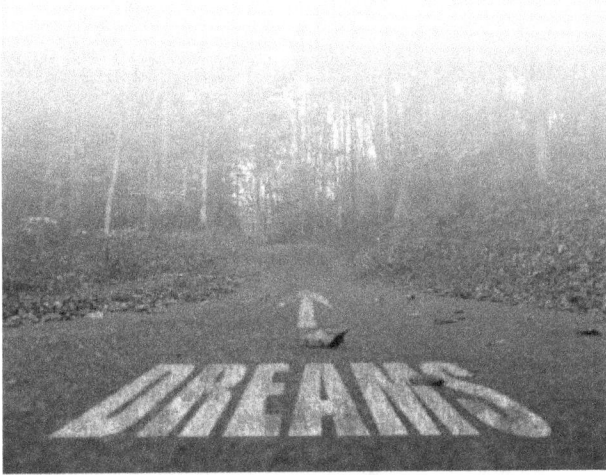

"Know the direction you want to go, and you won't lose sight of your dream."

-- Dr. Melissa Caudle

Without knowing your subject matter, it is exceedingly difficult to write a logline. However, I find it useful to develop my loglines before authoring my novel. The reason, a logline keeps me on the straight and narrow path in my journey. It provides me direction and focus.

I keep my loglines posted by my computer and refer to them often although I'm not married to them by any means. As I develop my novel, I usually rewrite my logline, which doesn't bother me. In fact, I find comfort in it. I know by the time I have completed writing the novel, my logline is honed. Loglines should benefit you, not deter you. Let them take shape, and they will shape your novel.

ACTIVITY

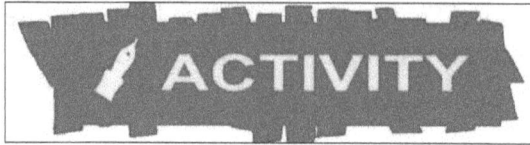

Re-write the following "Rejected" loglines according to the guidelines presented throughout this book.

Original Logline 1 – (semi-corrected for spelling.)

I have an idea for a reality show I want your company to produce. It is a reality show on me and the new life I created in New Orleans. I come here with my dog and cat and have found kindness in many peoples. I have always thought I should be my own reality show.

Extract the four elements from the statement.

Subject -- _____
Verb-- _____
Action Description -- _____
Outcome -- _____

Using the information, you abstracted, write an effective logline.

Logline 1

_____
_____
_____
_____

What would you name this novel?

Logline 2 - (semi-corrected for spelling, missing words etc.)

"I'll do anything on your show. I am a model, I am funny, and I'm a little crazy. It makes for a good time!"

Extract the four elements from the statement.

Subject -- _____
Verb -- _____
Action Description -- _____
Outcome -- _____

Using the information, you abstracted, write an effective logline.

Logline 2

_____
_____
_____
_____

What would you name the novel? _____

Answer Key: Answer will vary.

☻☻☻☻☻

79

ACTIVITY

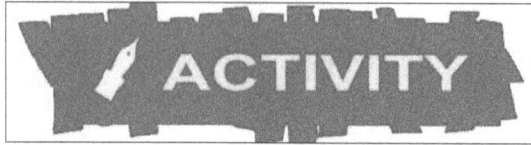

Now it is your turn to put what you've learned about writing loglines into action for your novel. Brainstorm five loglines for your book following the essential elements listed here. Keep them simple as you will continue to work to develop them.

Step One

Who is my novel about?

Subject -- _____

Ask: What is the action verb that best describes what your character or subject is doing? Refer to Appendix A for action verbs.

Verb -- _____

Ask: What is the subject doing?

Action Description -- _____

Ask: What does the subject learn or what changes does the subject make?

Outcome -- _____

Step Two

That was a good start. Now write a straightforward first draft of your novel's logline according to the placement of the elemental structures.

1. **Subject – Verb – Action - Outcome**

_____
_____
_____
_____

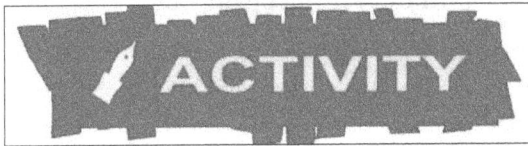

Enhance one of the loglines you created in the last activity with the enhancements indicated.

Logline 1 – Add an age to your subject.

_____
_____
_____
_____

Logline 2 – Give your main subject a name.

_____
_____
_____
_____

Logline 3 – Add a character trait to your main subject or character.

_____

_____

_____

_____

Logline 4 – Add adjectives to your action verb.

_____

_____

_____

_____

Logline 5 – Add an emotional journey.

_____

_____

_____

_____

Logline 6 – Add a crisis.

_____

_____

_____

_____

Logline 7 – Add the location.

_____

_____

_____

_____

Logline 8 – Add a Basic desire.

_____

_____

_____

_____

Logline 9 – Make your logline two sentences.

_____
_____
_____
_____
_____
_____
_____

Logline 10 – Make your logline three sentences.

_____
_____
_____
_____
_____
_____
_____

Logline 11 – Write your ultimate logline.

_____
_____
_____
_____
_____

Choose three out of the 11 loglines you have just written as your favorites and write them below. This time re-arrange the order of the subject, verb, action description and outcome.

Favorite Logline 1

_____
_____

_____

_____

Favorite Logline 2

_____

_____

_____

_____

Favorite Logline 3

_____

_____

_____

_____

Choose your favorite of the three loglines.

_____

_____

_____

_____

Using this logline, continue to modify and enhance it until you have a logline you love.

_____

_____

_____

_____

_____
_____
_____
_____

_____
_____
_____
_____

_____
_____
_____

_____
_____
_____

_____
_____
_____
_____

_____
_____
_____
_____

12. MULTIPLE LOGLINES FOR YOUR BOOK

"There's nothing better than an attention-grabbing logline to make me purchase a book"

-- Dr. Melissa Caudle

N ow what? You have learned the essential elements of a logline, you manipulated those that I wrote, and you have created your own. What are you going to do with them? There are a variety of ways to use your loglines.

- On a postcard to mail out to beta readers, bloggers, podcasters, and journalists.

- In a single-sentence logline book trailer.

- In a two-sentence logline book trailer.

- In the description for your ISBN.

- As part of your Amazon description.

- On your sell sheets.

- In different advertisement mediums.

- On your social media links when promoting your book.

- To pitch your book to a publisher.

- Use them above an excerpt on your website.

- To grab the attention of your reader, so they purchase your book.

NOTES

A Message from the Author

Dear Author:

Congratulations on honing your craft as an author. You should be immensely proud of yourself because writing a book takes lots of dedication, patience, skill, and time as does writing a compelling logline for it. Throughout this book, I mentioned several of my novels and used examples of the loglines from them, and because of that, I'm including excerpts from The *Keystroke Killer: Transcendence, Never Stop Running, A.D.A.M. The Beginning of Life,* and *Secret Romances: A Forbidden Thirst for Love.* Please enjoy as you read or listen to the excerpts.

Best regards,

Dr. Mel

AN EXCERPT FROM THE KEYSTROKE KILLER

New Orleans – 2058 - MATTHEW RAYMOND, a private investigator, locked into a maze of deceit and deception uncovers the truth of Project Transcendence.

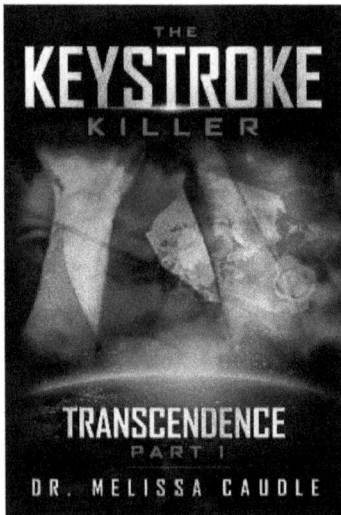

For Matthew Raymond, his job as a private investigator is personal. Extremely personal. After the disturbing 2053 murder of his sister Livia, Matthew left in a rage searches for her killer and answers to the mysterious questions that lurked around her death. Now years later, Matthew realizes his problems just went from bad to worse as he discovers himself immersed in a city where the wealthy and corrupt politicians rule. With his sister's murder still his focus, he finds himself in a cunning game of cat-and-mouse when he stumbles across The Keystroke Killer and uncovers a secret device capable of sending people to the fourth dimension without a trace. Project Transcendence becomes Matthew's new fixation. Searching the Deep South for answers, he uncovers family secrets, lies, corruption and a world on the brink of destruction. Can Matthew survive and save the world from the threat? Will he untangle the mystery of Livia's death? Find out in this compelling story, *The Keystroke Killer*.

AUDIOBOOK AVAILABLE

Written by Dr. Melissa Caudle

Narrated by Scott Ellis

THE KEYSTROKE KILLER: TRANSCENDENCE

Excerpt from Chapter 3

There's No Place Like Home

Matthew rose and kicked the chair beside him. "Damn it." *Why didn't I listen to her?*

The desk clerk slid open the frosted window divider. "Detective Raymond." She waited for a response. "Detective Raymond."

Matthew's eyes flushed. *If I'd only gotten there in time.*

"Detective Raymond!"

"I'm not a detective; I'm a private investigator." He approached the door that led to a hall.

"Good luck in there."

A loud hum released the locked door. He stepped through the uninviting invitation.

In the middle of the hall stood two additional armed guards. The area consisted of several recessed secured eight by ten-inch lockers, a checkpoint station, and an ironclad entry door that included an eye recognition keypad developed by Dimension Global. The door, dark gray metal six inches thick and eight feet tall, and how it sounded as it locked behind him made the biggest impression on Matthew over the last four years.

A loud buzzer, a clang, and a big bang echoed throughout the hall. Going out didn't sound as menacing. As he approached the guarded area, his heart raced, his temperature rose, and the tension throughout his entire body increased. He soon would sit across from the monster who killed his sister.

"Mr. Raymond, Check your weapon here." The husky guard remained alert as Matthew gently removed his gun from the holster.

"I know the drill." He handed it to him. "I don't like being unarmed."

The second guard pierced his eyes. "You don't have a choice if you want to visit Milo. Or, you could stop your yearly visitations."

"Not a chance. That shithead knows what happened to my sister. If it's the last thing I do, I'll beat the truth out of him."

"Don't you mean get the truth out of him?"

"Yea, that's what I meant. The bastard murdered my sister."

"Your sister was a victim of the Co-Ed serial killer? I thought you were the U.S. Marshall who captured him?"

"I should have killed him on the spot."

"Meaning, you could have?"

"Can I get on with this or am I the one being interrogated?"

The guard stepped to the retinal scan. The red light zipped across his eye and turned green. Click. The locker opened, and the guard secured Matthew's weapon.

Clang. The door slid into the recess of the wall giving way to the rancid urine smell and smeared dried fecal matter on the walls. The guards led Matthew down the unwelcoming hall. A faint whisper of burning flesh permeated from the left, the odor of carbolic soap from the staff restroom on the right, and the stench of unwashed clothes from the air vents filled the air.

Matthew looked at the visitor's restroom door. "I need to go in."

"Make it quick. Visiting hours are almost over."

***

The restroom door creaked as it shut behind him. Someone took a dump in the toilet and left it unflushed.

In the far corner by the janitor's closet, a rusty tin bucket served as the final resting place to an enormous and decomposed rat, which reeked of rotting decay stifling Matthew.

"Disgusting people." *Did they leave their manners and dignity outside the gate?* He shuffled to the sink and scrutinized his reflection wrinkled by torment. A tear fell from his left bloodshot eye as he thought of the exact moment Milo slaughtered his sister.

***

Milo clutched Livia's hair as he dragged her into the Army green public restroom at Kenner City Park. The pervasive odor of urine filled the air.

Matthew in hot pursuit retrieved his magnum and sprinted toward them. He raced into the bathroom high on angered emotion out of breath.

92

Milo held a machete against Livia's throat as he grinned sinisterly. "You made it in time to watch your sister die."

"Let go of her."

"If I let her go, you will kill me." Milo taunted him as he pressed the knife harder against Livia's throat. "And, if I don't let go, you will kill me. Either way, you lose."

"Let go now!" Matthew's muscles contracted to know the monster before him would take her life.

"What will big brother do? Save baby sis, or capture a serial killer?" His ice-cold stare of gunmetal gray prevailed.

"Both. I'll do both. Put the fucking knife down, and we all can walk away."

"Giving up your vow to serve and protect?" Milo taunted to get a rise out of Matthew. "You'd let me walk, if I let her go? I think not. I must protest."

"I'll kill you. Put down the knife and let her go."

"Too bad." Milo slit Livia's throat and shoved her to the ground. "You're too late, hesitation kills."

Matthew lunged to save Livia. He kneeled over her and tried to stop the sprouting blood from her neck with his hands pressed hard against the wound. "Livia." Her eyes rolled back; she took her last breath.

Milo snickered as he watched the loving embrace between a brother and a very bloody sister.

"You're a butcher. You'll pay for this!" Matthew lunged toward Milo and struck the cumbersome machete from his grip. He heaved him against the cracked roach-infested sink. Milo's cheek connected to it and split open. Blood smeared onto the sink and dripped down Milo's face. Matthew grabbed Milo by the shoulders and heaved his head against the mirror, which shattered into several pieces and crashed into the pool of Livia's blood.

Milo snatched a sharp mirror fragment, charged Matthew, stabbed him, and sliced his left shoulder.

Matthew glowered at him, bent to deliver a reverse round kick, but slipped on Livia's blood falling backward onto his butt.

Milo laughed as he held back his mental powers to provoke Matthew. "I'm just getting started."

Matthew bolted up, quick onto his feet, and delivered a round kick. His foot connected solidly into Milo's ribcage cracking several ribs.

Airborne, Milo, slammed against the wall. He grunted, took a deep breath, and charged Matthew.

Matthew outmaneuvered the serial killer. He dodged him, clutched Milo's shoulders, and used the momentum to propel him headfirst slamming him against the wall.

Bloody, Milo zigzagged toward Matthew.

Matthew rushed him, grabbed his shoulders, and butted his head against his forehead.

The room spun as Milo staggered toward his opponent. His eyes rolled into the back of his head, collapsing next to Livia.

Matthew kicked Milo's ribs. He yanked his handcuffs from the pouch so hard it busted his lip.

Milo groaned and barely opened one eye, more of a wink.

A drop of blood fell from Matthew's nose onto the back of Milo's bald, tattooed head. Matthew dropped to his knees and handcuffed him. "I have you now, you son of a bitch. You will rot in Hell for what you have done."

Matthew kneeled by his sister, checked her pulse, and closed her eyes, brushing his fingers across them. He stood and kicked Milo's face.

Police sirens blared as seconds ticked away.

Matthew glimpsed his bloody reflection in the mirror. He ambled to the sink and washed his face.

A light blue electrical power surge, originating at the overhead light fixture, radiated downwards onto the mirror, which captured his attention. The blue light pulsated, zipped through the running water, across the metal pipes, and onto the floor to Livia's blood. Livia shimmered a faint blue as the surge entombed her. She became transparent and vanished along with her crimson blood.

Matthew became faint as he felt Livia's life leave her body. "No!"

S.W.A.T. burst into the restroom, pointing their rifles toward Matthew. Matthew raised his hands above his head. A red laser dot centered on his forehead. Without lowering his hands, he pointed at the unconscious and bloody Milo. "That's the Co-Ed serial killer. Notify my father, Squad Commander of the New Orleans Police Intelligence Unit, Matthew Raymond."

***

Matthew exited the bathroom. The guard escorted him to the interview room at the end of the dreary hall. "You have ten minutes. Anything before that, knock on the door, and I'll let you out."

The nine by nine-foot room had a two-way mirror on the north wall. By mandate, Warden Stronghold and several guards watched the conversation between the rugged investigator and the ice-cold serial killer. The camera mounted high in the corner of the room reflected onto a bare bulb hung from the fourteen-foot ceiling.

Milo shackled at his feet and chained at his wrists sat on a metal stool behind a metal table. Both secured to the floor by bolts. A single wooden chair on the opposite side of the table near the door entrance awaited the interrogator.

When Matthew entered, Milo's hands pulled tight against the round metal restraint. He jerked the chains sneering at Matthew. "These necessary? I thought by now you and I understood each other."

Matthew didn't fall for the bait unaffected by Milo's threatening gesture or posturing and calmly sat. "Had is the operative word. Why should I trust you without them?"

"You're not dead, are you?" *I could kill you with one thought.*

"The chains stay."

"Then, I don't talk." *He's an idiot.*

A standoff ensued as neither the interrogator nor the killer wanted to retreat. Matthew maintained the upper hand confronting Milo. He sat stiffly. Milo followed suit. Neither man wanted to blink first as they glowered into each other's eyes. The silence roared until Matthew made the first move as he tussled his fingers through his scruffy uncombed hair. "Let me remind you of the position you're in. I put you here. I can keep you here."

The table vibrated as Milo scowled back unnerved. He responded to Matthew's emphatic statements by sneering more amused than intimidated. "That's supposed to make me talk?" Milo jerked toward the resolute Matthew. Only the chains that bound Milo prevented him from reaching his visitor.

Matthew didn't flinch. Not one recoil gave Milo the result he hoped.

"Oooo! I'm really scared now. Big brother needs protection by the chains that bind me. You're afraid to unchain me. Rightly so."

Matthew reached into his back pocket, grabbed a folded envelope, and pretended to hand it to the chained prisoner.

95

Milo gritted his teeth, grunted, and growled.

Matthew pretended not to notice as he dangled the envelope back and forth in front of Milo one inch out of his reach. "Open it."

"Not today." Milo desired to keep the upper hand.

"You scared of what you'll see?"

"Nothing in your show and tell game scares me." Milo extended his left middle finger and wiggled it.

A sneer crossed Matthew's lips; he didn't take the jeering bait as he placed the envelope onto the table out of Milo's reach. He flexed his fingers, folded his hands, and slowly placed them on the table. Matthew sat upright. "What I can show you should scare the piss out of you. It's from Nathan Hammer."

"You piqued my curiosity." Milo tried to slam his bound hands onto the table.

A lump formed in Matthew's throat as he secured the envelope between his thumb and index finger and lowered it one inch from Milo's shackled hands. "I'm not interested in what does or doesn't pique your interest." Matthew provoked Milo by fanning the envelope.

Unnerved, Milo deepened his cold stone stare, remained motionless fighting the urge to use his telepathic ability to suck air from Matthew's lungs.

The chair scraped across the floor as Matthew rose. "Maybe next time you'll show me respect and play my show and tell game as you emphatically called it." He strode to the door.

Milo sneered as he chomped his teeth to taunt him.

Matthew used his knuckles and tapped on the door protruding his middle finger. "Up yours."

Tap. Tap. Tap.

Unamused and unaffected by Matthew's blatant gesture, Milo leered toward Matthew. "Watch your back. That's, if you can."

"Meaning?"

"You couldn't watch your sister's. Now could you?"

Matthew turned toward Milo as his eyes trickled the calculated insolence of his stare. "You're not allowed to talk about my sister." He spewed spit with each angered word.

"You should have seen her face when I slit her throat." Milo gloated him further. "Oh, excuse me. You did." His tone in Joker fashion more befitting a character in *Batman* seemed to bounce in the room against the walls. "Such a thing of beauty to feel as her body jerked going limp before her last breath. Big brother couldn't save little sister." Milo smirked and tilted his head to the side. "I remember her sweet perfume and the silkiness of her hair." A grin of wry amusement dashed across his lips.

Matthew bolted toward Milo, grabbed the villain's head, and slammed it against the table. Blood oozed from Milo's nose. He pressed Milo's bloody face relentlessly on the table as if he had the strength of a Western lowland gorilla from the jungles of Africa. "You son of a bitch!"

Milo strained to avert Matthew's glare. His yellow stained teeth bloody.

"Where did my sister go?"

Milo's blank stare enraged an already violent Matthew.

"How did you make her vanish?" Matthew slammed Milo's head against the table over and over.

"Lost control big brother? I think so."

"You son of a bitch."

"That's the only name you have left in your arsenal? Low on vocabulary for a Tulane graduate."

Matthew slammed Milo's head three more times against the already bloody surface. "How's this for vocabulary? You're demonic."

Three guards rushed into the room and restrained Matthew. To break free, Matthew thrashed in their arms to escape from the three-person hold.

Milo licked the blood from his lips and sat up. "Tastes like your sister's."

DR. MELISSA CAUDLE

A.D.A.M.

By Dr. Melissa Caudle

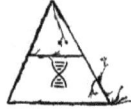

A scientist. An alien lifeform. A secret base.

Consequences for Mankind.

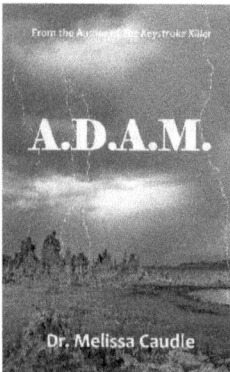

Meet Dr. Sandra Eve Bradford, an astrobiological researcher in charge of the A.D.A.M. Extraction Team who discovered a microbe that thrives off arsenic on the bottom of Mono Lake in California. General Anbar, Chief in Charge of the U.S. National Defense, orders his team to confiscate the samples and her research.

Dr. Bradford enlists her fellow researchers, Dr. Gregory Peterson, and her undergraduate assistant, Jessica Parker, to retrieve a new sample which set off a series of events and consequences.

In a government research facility, the microbe transformed into something alien. Once it becomes apparent to General Anbar the life form presents a national security risk, he orders his men to kidnap Dr. Bradford and holds her captive in an underground facility to continue her research.

The lifeform over a seven-day stretch, morphs into a human-like lifeform aging every moment toward death. His journey makes him question - What is life? What is love? What is hate? And, is there a God? This a story of possibilities and raises the questions - Are we alone in the universe? What else could be out there?

AVAILABLE IN PAPERBACK, EBOOK, AND AUDIOBOOK
Audiobook narrated by Rebecca Roberts

A.D.A.M.

Excerpt

CHAPTER TWO – TRUTH

Dr. Bradford drove her hunter green Fiat on Interstate 10 from New Orleans towards Slidell.

Jessica twisted her long brunette hair into a bun and secured it with a pink scrunchy. "I'm hungry. I'm not waiting any longer to eat." She dug through a white fast-food paper sack that rested in her lap, retrieved a breakfast sandwich, and unwrapped it. The odor permeated through the car. Jessica curled her nose. "The eggs smell rotten."

"Get over it. Nothing has smelled good to you since you took in that mouthful of salty water at Mono Lake."

Jessica gagged, crumpled her breakfast sandwich back into the wrapper and threw it back into the paper bag. "You can eat yours if you want, I'll wait for lunch."

Dr. Bradford darted her eyes over at Jessica. "Give me mine."

Jessica dug through the bag and retrieved another wrapped breakfast sandwich and handed it over.

Dr. Bradford unwrapped it, took one bite and spit it immediately back into the wrapper.

"Told you, but, no! You didn't believe me."

"Please be quiet; let me think."

The silence between them ensued as they crossed the bridge over Lake Pontchartrain.

Jessica leaned toward the dash to stretch her back. "Are you sure it's safe to go to the lab?"

"They can't kill me in public; so, I believe it's safe."

"It makes me nervous. Let's listen to Stephen Stone Diamond. He's talking about extraterrestrials today."

"That's what we need, an alien conspiracy."

"I thought that's what we're in now." Jessica pressed the radio's knob. "It's not working."

"That's the best news I've had all day."

Jessica grabbed her phone and opened her blog radio app.

". . . Not just life here on earth, but also extraterrestrial life." Stephen Stone Diamond's deep and golden voice enhanced the mysterious topic. "It is unknown if there is any connection to the mysterious deaths of Dr. Gregory Peterson and the late husband of Dr. Sandra Bradford, Dr. Jeffrey Peck, who were both members of N.A.E.T. For those of you who don't know what N.A.E.T. is, I will gladly inform my listeners. It is a branch of NASA and stands for National Astrobiological Extraction Team. Coincidently, the research team led by Dr. Sandra Bradford. Phone lines are open."

Dr. Bradford slammed her fist onto the dashboard. "Damn! It's out on Blog radio."

"I'm Stephen Stone Diamond. I'll be right back to take your calls."

Dr. Bradford clenched her jaw. "Turn it off. I don't care to listen."

Jessica grabbed her earbuds. "That's exciting. E. T. phone home. I got to call in."

"Like hell, you will."

Jessica secured her earbuds, dialed the blog radio number, and waited. "I'm on hold."

"Jessica. Hang up. You can't bring attention to yourself or to me. Now hang up."

"So why are you doing a press conference?"

"The public needs to know the truth about my research. If the public gets wind of what I've discovered, they'll demand the truth."

"Well, in my opinion, that is exactly what Stephen Stone Diamond will do."

"Jessica!"

❀

NASA Astrobiology Institute between the Louisiana and Mississippi border provided not only jobs but also fundamental research. From the spacecraft and booster shuttle rocket, the entry to the multi-functional compound reflected the nation's attitude about space exploration. Everyone wore either an official NASA or N.A.E.T. employee badge representing they worked either as an independent scientist on the National Astrobiological Extraction Team or a part of NASA. Visitors must sign in and wear visitor badges on their lapels too.

Dr. Bradford rushed toward the three-story "Carl Sagan Astrobiology Lab" which housed the N.A.E.T. lab. Behind her, Jessica, Rebecca Newcombe, and George, a camera operator quickly followed.

Without provocation, Dr. Bradford collided into Dr. Phyllis Gordon, a forty-four American scientist, and Dr. Edward Stolz, a fifty-two German scientist. Rebecca motioned for George to roll the camera.

Dr. Gordon's eyes pierced toward Dr. Bradford's. "You've gathered quite a following since our discovery."

"I'd have to agree."

"Too bad our samples were confiscated."

"This isn't the time nor the place to discuss this." Dr. Bradford strode briskly toward the N.A.E.T. research building.

The entourage followed as Rebecca motioned for George to continue to roll the camera. "What was all that about?" She caught up with Dr. Bradford.

"Common professional jealousy. That's all there is to it."

Jessica frowned. "I think not. It's about..."

"...Loose lips sink ships." Dr. Bradford motioned using her fingers as if locking a key for Jessica to close her mouth.

Jessica confirmed when she moved her fingers across her lips as if zipping a zip-lock baggy.

Rebecca glowered toward George. "Cut the camera. Damn it!"

The entourage barged into the N.A.E.T. building.

❀

The morning sun reflected off the five test tubes of murky water which rested on one of the lab's counters. A microscopic particle floated inside one test tube and for a nanosecond glowed neon yellow.

Moments later, the entourage entered Dr. Bradford's lab. Jessica flipped on the lights as she wrinkled her nose and smelled the faint musky and sulfur smell. "I'll never forget this smell."

The well-equipped lab included beakers, flasks, a Liebig condenser, and graduated cylinders showed the lab's importance. Most prominent, a silver and white 60X-2599X-2 binocular turret professional biological microscope proved essential in isolating micro-organisms. In the corner, an assortment of lab experiments and three twenty-five-gallon tanks filled from the murky waters retrieved from several lakes labeled Lake Pontchartrain, Grand Isle and Honey Island Swamp filled the area. On the wall above the door a twelve-inch round battery-operated clock and a sign - "A.D.A.M. Extraction Team" marked the entrance to the lab. Each white cabinet had stainless steel handles, which enhanced the sterile environment.

Rebecca tapped George onto his shoulder. "Be sure to capture everything in the lab. I want lots of B-Roll."

Dr. Bradford and Jessica dressed into their white lab coats, proceeded to the sink, and washed their hands.

Jessica prepped a microscope and a sterile slide. "I'll make sure everything is ready Dr. B."

"Perfect, Jessica. Just follow the protocol. We have to get this correct." Dr. Bradford stepped to a locked cabinet, retrieved a bottle of arsenic and an eyedropper, and placed the items next to the microscope onto the lab counter. "Rebecca, it won't take much longer to set up."

"That's good to know. I don't have much longer."

Dr. Bradford retrieved the test tube, which contained the particle. She extracted a sample as Jessica handed her the glass microscope slide. Dr. Bradford placed three drops of the murky liquid onto the sterile slide.

Jessica lifted her brow with excitement. "Isn't this amazing?"

Rebecca's frown deepened. "That's it, a test tube full of murky water and three drops on a slide."

Dr. Bradford defended her actions. "It's evidence that challenges the way we think and view life as we know it."

Jessica handed another test tube to Dr. Bradford. She filled the container using the water sample and gave the vial back to her. "Jessica, mark this sample A."

"Yes, Ma'am." Jessica looked at Rebecca. "It's in there. I've seen it."

Again, Dr. Bradford's posture became defensive. "You can't see it without the aid of a microscope." She filled the second vial and handed it to Jessica.

"Sample B." Jessica nodded with pride.

Dr. Bradford confirmed with a nod. "Remember, at its current state it is a microbe." She placed the prepared slide beneath the microscope as everyone observed and focused the microscope.

"I'll prepare the boiling water." Jessica predicted what Dr. Bradford would want as it had become standard procedure in the lab. She briskly strode across the room, filled a tea kettle, and set it onto the single electrical coil burner. She walked away but quickly returned to turn the knob to the on position.

As Dr. Bradford viewed the microbe under the powerful microscope, it vibrated and morphed into Dr. Bradford's eye. She lifted from the microscope, blinked, and rubbed her eyes.

Jessica noticed. "Something wrong Dr. B?"

"Nothing, an eyelash was in my eye." Dr. Bradford peered through the microscope and adjusted the focus again.

Rebecca's patience grew thin. "How did you obtain these samples? I thought the government confiscated them."

Dr. Bradford exhaled. "A few more seconds... There you are, look." Dr. Bradford stepped to the side as Rebecca stepped to the microscope. She glanced at Dr. Bradford before she lowered to view the microbe.

Dr. Bradford rubbed her neck. "Jessica, hand me my notebook, please."

Jessica strode to Dr. Bradford's desk, retrieved a brown leather journal, and strutted to Dr. Bradford and handed it over.

The tea kettle whistled. Jessica at once prepped a beaker of hot boiling water and brought it to Dr. Bradford.

Dr. Bradford handed her journal back to Jessica and then placed five drops of arsenic into the beaker.

Rebecca peered through the microscope. "Honestly, I see nothing."

Dr. Bradford exhaled in disappointment. "My best hypothesis is the microbe transitions as fast as I isolate it. I'll isolate it again for you."

The two women exchanged places. Dr. Bradford once again adjusted the microscope settings.

"You never answered my question. How did you obtain these samples?"

"Let's suffice it to say I was on the extraction team and managed to keep a sample for further study."

"You stole it?"

Jessica came to Dr. Bradford's defense. "We didn't steal it. We went..."

Dr. Bradford lifted from the microscope long enough to glare toward Jessica and twisted her fingers as if locking a door.

Jessica put her hand over her mouth as she lifted her brows.

Rebecca, annoyed at the silent gesture, huffed. "You agreed you would tell me everything." She gazed harshly at Dr. Bradford.

"I promised you an exclusive interview for a no question asked policy. When the time is right, we'll reveal our evidence and our source as to how we obtained another sample."

"I'll get another Emmy."

"I'll surely get my doctorate."

Dr. Bradford gave Jessica another cold glance.

"Well, I will. Won't I?"

The lab became uncomfortably silent as Dr. Bradford continued to isolate the microbe.

Rebecca tapped her foot. "Anytime would be ideal. I have a deadline for tonight's news."

"Patience, I almost have the microbe isolated."

"Yes, Dr. B always tells me that patience is a virtue."

"We go live at six. After the murder of your husband and Dr. Peterson, the world is waiting with bated breath to hear from the now infamous Dr. Sandra Bradford."

A reflective sadness came over Dr. Bradford, but she regained her professional composure. "You sound skeptical, Rebecca."

"Wouldn't you be? You claim to have evidence of an alien life form."

"Don't forget about me. I've seen it. Be sure to add that to your story. You know how to spell my name, right?"

Rebecca rolled her eyes. "This sounds ripe for a sci-fi murder mystery for *The Twilight Zone* and not the headline news story I wanted to break."

"I've isolated it; be quick this time." Dr. Bradford backed away from the microscope.

Rebecca quickly assumed her position and peered it as she squinted her left eye. "Like before, nothing."

"Maybe you don't know what you're looking for."

"Insults I don't need and won't tolerate."

"I didn't mean it to demean you. I apologize if I came across that way."

"Let's talk about the murders of your associates."

"I can't speak to the murders. I can only comment about the great men taken from this world. I was shocked to learn my husband was involved in a head-on collision, and it was an accident. The investigators ruled there was no foul play involved. Frankly, I'm horrified Dr. Peterson was gunned down while on a boating vacation on the same lake where we made our discovery."

Jessica bit her lower lip and paced. *I don't like the way this is going.*

"Doesn't this frighten you?" Rebecca swallowed and leered toward Dr. Bradford with unashamed confidence.

"Of course, I am as anyone in my situation would be. You never know who your enemy is, even if they stood in front of you as a friend. It's a cut-throat industry when claiming a scientific discovery."

"Especially one that's as big as this." Jessica beamed with delight.

A quiet knock on the lab's door caught everyone's attention.

Dr. Bradford looked at the samples and over toward the door as Jessica jumped and dropped Dr. Bradford's journal as a wallet-size photograph of an infant tumbled from it and onto the floor.

FBI Agent Morrison, a handsome African American male, late forties, and Agent Turner, an African American female in her late thirties, brashly entered.

Jessica's eyes widened as her trembling hands went straight toward the ceiling. "Whoa, gun!"

Agent Morrison flashed his shield. "Miss, you can put your hands down. We're here to speak to Dr. Bradford. I'm FBI Special Agent Morrison, and this is my partner, Special Agent Turner."

Jessica slowly placed her hands to her thighs as she glanced at the journal and the photograph. She retrieved the journal and set the photograph back inside the journal.

Dr. Bradford stepped forward. "I'm Dr. Bradford. How may I be of assistance?"

Agent Turner stepped forward. "Not in the presence of others. What we have to say is confidential. Everyone needs to leave, but Dr. Bradford."

Agent Morrison put his hand in front of his face and grabbed George's camera with the other. "Stop filming. You're in that directive too."

George jerked his camera out of Agent's Morrison's hands and stepped backward to put distance between them.

Jessica stomped her foot. "You're telling me, you barge into our lab and ask us to leave."

"We're not asking." His stare, as cold as ice, seemed menacing.

"But, I'm her graduate assistant."

"I have Freedom of the Press on my side." Rebecca stood steadfast.

Dr. Bradford raised her hand chest high. "Wait, anything I have to say, they can hear."

Agent Turner stepped closer toward Dr. Bradford. "In that case, you leave us no choice but to take you to FBI headquarters. Please, Dr. Bradford, retrieve your belongings and come with us. It will be easier for all involved."

A silent standoff prevailed.

"I'll consent, but I want it documented that I am cooperating." Dr. Bradford gathered her belongings and headed for the door.

Rebecca motioned for George to follow. He pursued the agents and Dr. Bradford as they exited from the lab.

"Wait! Dr. Bradford, your journal." Jessica handed over the journal.

Dr. Bradford hesitated. "You keep it. Jessica, lock down the lab. Use protocol FRIC."

"FRIC?" Agent Turner's brow creased. "And, that is code for what?"

"Factual Research Investigative Control."

Jessica smirked in agreement. "Lock up the science experiment to avoid contamination. FRIC that!"

Agent Morrison looked at Dr. Bradford. "Come with us, please."

The two agents escorted Dr. Bradford from the lab as Rebecca, George, and Jessica chased after them. The door shut behind them.

In a few seconds, Jessica re-entered the lab and secured the samples. The murky water in one of the five tubes glowed neon yellow as the water vibrated around it.

She retrieved her cell phone and dialed.

NEVER STOP RUNNING

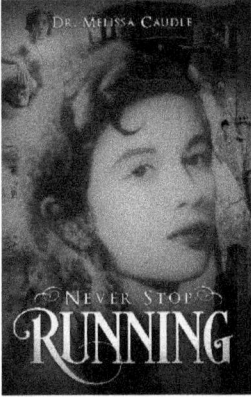

Based on a true story of one woman's struggle to recover her memories after a devastating accident left her with retrograde amnesia, "Never Stop Running" is an astonishing novel from an unforgettable author and is a must-read. What happens when the unthinkable occurs? What would you do if your loved one suddenly woke up and didn't know who you were or for that matter who your family was either? For David and Jackie Hennessey, they had the perfect white picket fence life, marriage, family, and careers until the unthinkable happened - an accident that left Jackie with no memory. The couple struggled to find a balance between what they once shared and their new life. After David discovered Dr. Grayson, a well-known regression hypnotherapist, he convinced Jackie to seek his services to retrieve her repressed memories. During her sessions, her memories surfaced only to uncover her past lives, which crisscross centuries in her mental time travel. Faced with a moral dilemma of believing the dreams were once a reality and twisting her religious convictions on reincarnation, Jackie questioned her sanity and feared for her life after seeing her deaths in her previous lives. She believed she could never stop running as her marriage degrades and falls apart. Based on real events of hypnotic regression sessions of one brave woman, this is a tale of destiny and soul mates not to be missed. The most intriguing book you'll read all year. You don't have to believe in reincarnation to enjoy this tale, but it will get you to thinking about the possibility.

AVAILABLE IN PAPERBACK, EBOOK, AND AUDIOBOOK

Audiobook narrated by Jessie Drumm

Excerpt from *Never Stop Running*

1. OPEN THE DOOR

Dr. Grayson sat in a Victorian chair; his eyes focused on Jackie, who lay in a deep hypnotic state on a worn royal blue velvet chaise. The scar which ridged from her scalp to below her cheek covered by make-up embarrassed Jackie as she leaned her face against the pillow to hide it.

"From this point on, when I say sleep and snap my fingers, you will remember this state and go to it. Now breathe in and out." Dr. Grayson drew a deep breath.

Jackie responded to his suggestion with a huge-heaved sigh of relief.

"Jackie, I'm going to ask you a series of questions. You will not awaken but stay in this peaceful state. You will remain aware of your surroundings. Noises won't bother you. You will only respond to my voice. Do you understand?"

"Yes."

"Jackie, search through your past and find a door and enter." Dr. Grayson observed Jackie's body language and eye movement beneath her eyelids, giving her time to select a door. "Do you see the door?"

"I don't know which one to enter."

"The choice is yours. Think of a time in your past and open the door."

Her eyelids fluttered, her facial muscles flattened, and she looked more mannequin than human. Her right index finger lifted. "That one."

Dr. Grayson shook his head in approval. "That's great, Jackie, open the door and step through. Where are you?"

"I'm in a scary place. I feel cold. It's really cold... dark... It's misty."

"Nothing can harm you, Jackie; you're safe. What are you doing in this place?"

"I'm in a dark alley."

"Are you alone?"

She barely shook her head. "Someone else is here... He's calling a woman's name."

In his hypnotherapist mind, Dr. Grayson analyzed her statement. "What name?"

"Gertrude."

"What is Gertrude doing?"

∞

Gertrude, age twenty-three, dressed in an 1880s overcoat with a silver-fox fur collar and an 1880s hat, ran down a dark alley lit only by the orange glow of the oil street lamps and the blood moon. Fog graced the area as a light mist sprinkled. She tried to catch her breath. Smoke from the heat of her breath clashed with the cold misty night air.

A large man who wore a black Gothic cape chased her. "Gertrude! Stop! You'll never get away with this."

Gertrude ran to escape him. She tripped and fell scrapping both knees; the ground ripped her silk stockings. With the man in close pursuit, she pushed herself up and ran. She lengthened her stride as she looked over her shoulder.

Within an arm's-length of her, the man gained ground; he swiftly closed in. He lifted a butcher knife, lunged at her, and pierced her through her back.

Her body lurched forward as she fell in slow motion and landed in a mud puddle face down. The clammy chill of death gripped her.

He kneeled, rolled her over, and jerked her brass crystal domed watch pendant from around her neck. She heaved as she took her last breath.

∞

Jackie raised her hips, wiggled her shoulders, and exhaled.

"Relax Jackie, he can't harm you; you're safe."

Jackie jolted. "He killed Gertrude; I saw him kill her." Jackie heavily breathed as her heart pounded against her ribcage.

"Jackie, what year did Gertrude die?"

"October eleventh, eighteen seventy-nine."

He pondered the date. "All right, Jackie, let's move somewhere else. I want you to think of a calm, peaceful place, a beautiful place."

Jackie bolted up with her eyes wide opened. She put her hand on her forehead and heaved. "I don't want to do this."

"Please know you made extreme progress."

"I'm finished for today; I want to go home."

"Jackie, remember your subconscious has a way to deal with your fears if you allow it."

Jackie's voice cracked as emotions flowed. "It's just overwhelming." Jackie cleared her throat and held back her tears.

"I understand. Sometimes when we witness past events, we can become confused and scared. This is a normal process."

"I don't understand what just happened." A tear rolled down her mascara-smeared-scared face. "Who did I see die?

To be continued

Available on Amazon

Never Stop Running Dream Journal
Never Stop Running Regression Journal

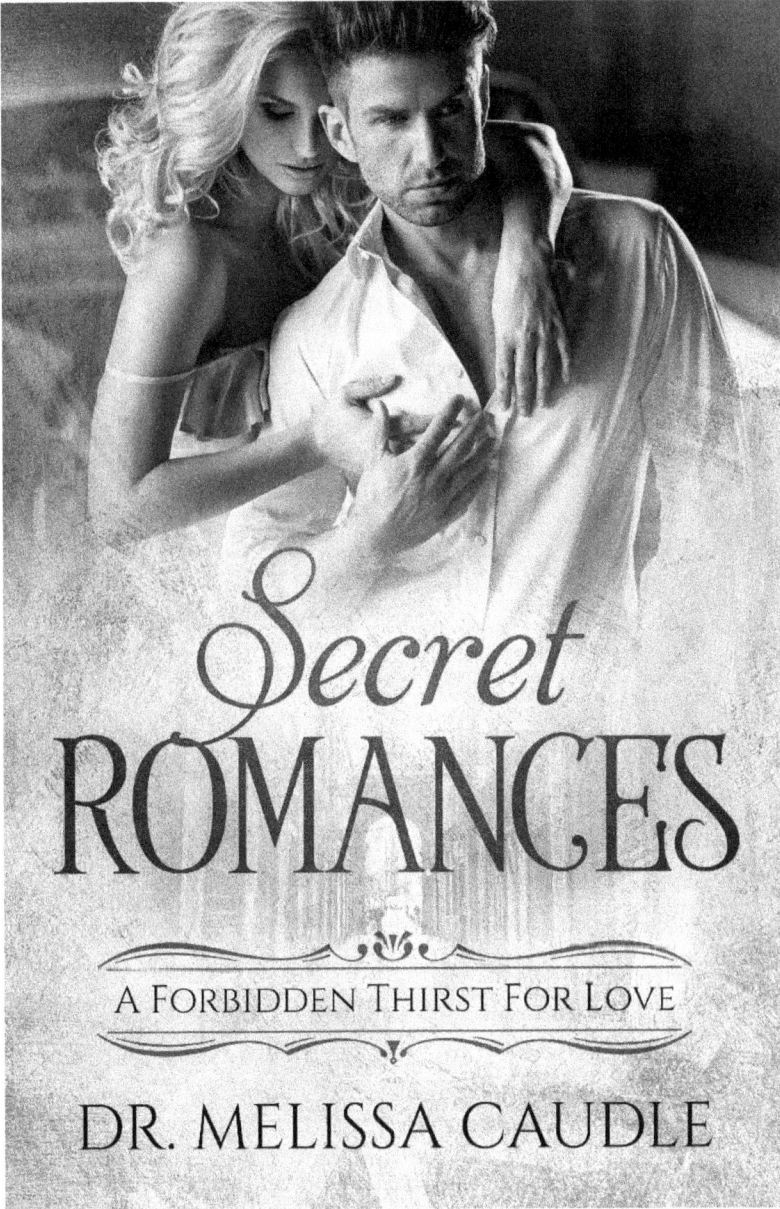

Secret
ROMANCES

A FORBIDDEN THIRST FOR LOVE

DR. MELISSA CAUDLE

COMING SUMMER 2020

CHAPTER ONE

Fate

The downtown district of New Orleans, Louisiana bubbled with excitement along Canal Street. The morning autumn brisk air swept through Angela Whitford's long blonde hair as she made her way down the crowded sidewalk through the morning commuters. Everything about her said, a wealthy socialite, as she clutched onto her black leather messenger's bag in one hand and held her cellphone to her ear with the other. "I completely take that as a compliment, Dad. Your faith in me is what I always wanted. Take note the magazine hasn't fallen apart, and it's been four days since you turned it over to me."

From the way she strode toward the entrance of a high rise building to her prestigious Armani royal blue suit, she exuded confidence. Heads turned as she passed. Although forty-years-old, she didn't look a day over thirty. "Thank you, Dad. You don't have to worry. You and mom enjoy your world cruise. For the last time, I can handle the magazine. You've groomed me for this position since I could first read."

Angela stopped on the corner of Royal Street and gazed toward the sky rise building. A huge confident grin touched her lips. "Of course, Dad, if anything goes wrong, I'll notify you immediately." She took a deep breath as she pressed the end button on her cell phone.

The heavy morning traffic always provided a challenge to cross the street. In the distance, streetcar 941 approached. *I always have loved our streetcars.* She patiently waited amid the others as they tightly squeezed in around her at the crosswalk. She waited for the walking signal to flash white; and when it did, she scarpered into the crosswalk lane increasing her path toward her destination. The crowd on the corner seemed like one as they crossed.

A man in a Blue Bayou Cleaning jumpsuit approached and collided into Angela, knocking her possessions out of her hands. His blue eyes, black hair and masculine jawline made him exceptionally handsome. "Lady, I'm sorry. Let me help you." He flashed an apologetic grin.

She drilled the man with a penetrating stare. "I think you've already helped." Her angry tone gave way to a brief smile at the corner of her lips when her blue eyes met his.

He quickly gathered her belongings and handed them to her. "Again, lady, I'm very sorry."

Several horns blew as the red light changed to green. An elderly driver stuck his head out of the car window with a glare of pure fury. "Hey, move out of the way!"

Angela face contorted to one of stunned surprise. "I guess we are blocking traffic."

He nodded and shot a wink in her direction. "Have a good day ma'am."

Honk! Honk! "Move it, lady!"

The man in the Blue Bayou jumpsuit strode quickly to the opposite side of the street. Angela clutched her belongings and dashed toward the high-rise building. She glanced at her crystal diamond Rolex watch. *I can't be late. There's too much riding on this.* She increased her pace sprinting through the rotating glass doors and into the building. The marble floors and golden brass trim glistened from the morning's sun.

The security guard smiled. "Good morning Ms. Whitford."

"Good morning, Charles." She briskly strode to the elevator and pressed the up-arrow button repeatedly. "Come on; I don't have all day."

Other businesspeople gathered around and waited too. Everyone seemed in a hurry for their workday to begin.

Finally, the elevator door slid open. Several people hurriedly exited as she waited for it to empty. She stepped in and pressed the button for floor twenty-three as several other others entered crowding the elevator like packed sardines. Angela quickly scooted to the back and leaned against the back mirrored wall.

The elevator doors shut and smoothly ascended, stopping on the fifth floor. Six people exited. Angela stepped forward and snippily pressed the close button several times. The elevator door, slow to close, made Angela huff as she pushed the close button again.

The man who stood next to her frowned. "You know that doesn't speed things up."

"It might not, but it makes me feel better."

"Enough said." He stared straight ahead at the door as did she.

The elevator stopped on the eleventh floor. The man exited. "Have a great day. Go ahead and press that button since it makes you feel better."

Angela smirked. "What a jerk." The people's eyes darted her way. "Sorry, but he's a jerk."

After several more stops, the elevator finally reached the twenty-third floor. When the door opened, Angela exited immediately stepping into a lavish foyer. In the center, a forty-two-inch mahogany table that displayed a massive fresh floral orchid arrangement showcased the elegance of the office. She gazed at the impressive silver and royal blue inlaid 3D signage for *Elite* magazine behind the reception desk. An I'm-the-boss-now-smile pursed her lips. The floor to ceiling windows provided a perfect view of the city below.

She passed Monique, age twenty-four, a blue-eyed quirky, beautiful red-haired receptionist, who wore a Michael Kors navy blue cap sleeve stud trim Ponte dress. "Good morning, Ms. Whitford. You have several messages that I gave to your secretary."

"Thank you, Monique."

"My pleasure."

Angela made her way through the busy cubicle journalist area, which buzzed as if in the stock market exchange. By the size of the workspace and the number of cubicles at least thirty people had started their fast-paced workday with publishing deadlines to meet.

Katie Summers, age thirty-four, and senior journalist stood as Angela passed. "Excuse me, Ms. Whitford. I have the article on the Smyth and Smyth Architect firm completed; I look forward to your feedback."

"I'll get to it as soon as possible."

Katie shrugged in disappointment and sat.

Angela continued her pace toward her office as several of her employees who stood on the side engaged in conversation either greeted her or froze in place as if they did something wrong when she passed.

Francis Murphy, a beautiful brunette, age thirty-three, dressed in a Kasper sleek black dress and black heels, met Angela as she approached her corner office, which overlooked the Mississippi River. The plaque on the door read -- "Angela Whitford – Senior-Vice President."

Angela stopped short of entering. "When is my nameplate going to be updated? I'm the CEO now."

"Hopefully, today ma'am."

"Good. Please follow up on that."

"I'll make it my priority."

The women scurried into Angela's private office decorated exquisitely in teal and white as if on Fifth Avenue in a posh New York building. From the elegant glass desk to the sumptuous leather teal chairs, the office exuberated wealth and stature. When she sat, the Mississippi River Bridge loomed behind her.

"Ms. Whitford, a quick update. Your ten o'clock meeting with Mr. Morgan has been rescheduled due to a family emergency. I took the liberty to schedule another meeting with a new client."

"You did this without checking with me. You know I vet all our potential advertisers. We have a prestigious clientele. Not everyone can purchase ads in our magazine."

"I must confess, I did. However, it is for John Legions of Legions Airlines. Does he need to be vetted?"

Angela sighed. "I guess not, but don't make that a habit."

"Yes, ma'am. Are you ready for your interview with KWNC this morning?"

"I forgot about that. Of all days, why today? We have a publishing deadline."

"I believe it has something to do with you making the top list of the most influential businesswomen in Louisiana. Now that your CEO of one of the nation's top magazines, everyone wants to know everything about you besides being just a socialite."

"I get it, but I don't have time for this. I don't need to be marketed. If I wanted that, I'd put an ad in my magazine."

"Like you always say, there's no such thing as bad press."

"Fine, just give me a heads up before they prance into my office."

"Consider it done."

***

George Sidwell Preparatory Senior High school's gymnasium filled quickly with students sporting their red and black school colors as they made their way into the bleachers. At the end of the basketball court, four rows of chairs filled by the football team waited patiently for the pep rally to begin. Preston Alcott Billiford III, blonde hair and hazel eyes, sat on the front row sporting his number nine quarterback jersey.

At the opposite end, the band played the school fight song as the majorettes and flag team performed.

In one section of the bleachers sat the nominees for homecoming queen; each wore a magnificent mum with ribbons glittered with the words – "Homecoming Court."

Mr. Hayes, the sixty-year-old with silver hair principal, high-fived several students as they entered.

Lonnie, a senior, looked more like a gothic-punk rock star in a school uniform than someone who attended an elite private school sat midway in the bleacher section next to his best friend, Conrad Pierce, who also identified with the gothic-punk style. Conrad elbowed Lonnie. "I don't know what you see in her. Besides, don't you think she's out of our social class?"

Lonnie's brows creased. "Just because she's not rich doesn't mean I can't date her."

"I still don't see what you see in her. You're from old-school money; her family is dirt-bottom broke. The only reason she is here is because of the scholarship she received. I think they call that integration."

"Conrad, you sound like a snob."

"That's because I probably am. Like my daddy always said, it is just as easy to fall in love with someone rich as it is to fall in love with someone poor."

"You're a snob. When you get to know Jamie, you'll understand."

"I'm just saying, save yourself. You'll find a girl more suited to your ranking when you go to Harvard next year. You at least owe yourself that much."

The band's song ended as the flag team and majorettes took their seats on the bleachers.

Conrad exhaled. "Please pray that the Glee Club doesn't perform."

"Since when do you pray?"

"At the thought of the Glee Club. I'll take rock and roll any day of the week."

"Here they come." Lonnie pointed to the girl's locker room exit.

The cheerleading squad sprinted into the gym, screaming, "Go Spartans!" Three male cheerleaders and the team's Spartan mascot dashed from the boy's locker room. Several cheerleaders performed backflips until they lined up in formation across center court. The mascot strutted his way in front of the bleachers as his red cape flowed. His fake gold Spartan helmet almost fell off as he grabbed it.

Conrad elbowed Lonnie again and then pointed at the mascot. "I wouldn't dress like that even if they gave me a million dollars. Oh, wait. I already have a million dollars. I'm a trust fund baby."

"Now I know you're a snob."

"A rich snob, but what male in their right mind wears a gladiator dress exposing his hairy ass legs? He looks ridiculous."

"You're one to talk. Have you noticed we don't exactly fit in either?"

"It's not because we can't. It's because we don't want to."

Conrad raised a rocker fist pump. "Rock on!"

Lonnie smiled at waved at Jamie Seamore, a seventeen-year-old senior with long curly brunette hair, green eyes, who held the position of head cheerleader. She stopped at center court several feet in front of the squad.

Jamie took her position as she quickly glanced at the other squad members. "Ready? Okay!"

The squad performed a cheer, which included Jamie as the flyer at the end of the stunt. She flipped off backward, landing in the male cheerleader's arms.

Lonnie never took his eyes off Jamie as the squad cheered their way to a dance formation.

"Is she still pressuring you about going to the homecoming dance tonight?"

"I've got it handled."

"I'm just saying, if you give in now, you'll always have to give in. Set your precedents early in a relationship."

"This explains a lot. It's clear why you don't have a girlfriend."

"I don't want one. I'm waiting for the finer women to come my way. It's called college woman."

Lonnie cupped his hands over his mouth. "Go, Jamie!"

Conrad elbowed Lonnie again. "Please don't embarrass yourself. Let's get out of here."

As the squad performed their dance routine, Lonnie and Conrad exited the gym.

Jamie's animated cheerleader demeanor momentarily faded as her eyes followed Lonnie.

***

Angela, self-assured in her stance, stood in front of the floor to ceiling window in the journalist cubicle area. A few feet away, Francis observed as she wrote down every question Houston Meadows, a handsome KWNC male reporter, asked of her boss as his camera operator filmed.

"Ms. Whitford, one last question. How do you intend to keep the magazine's reputation now that your father has retired?"

Angela bumptiously pursed her lips. "My father would not have put me in this position if I wasn't ready. I have worked here for this magazine since I was sixteen. I started by scrubbing toilets. I delivered the mail. I served as a receptionist. I sold advertisements. I copy-edited. I wrote articles. My father made sure I understood every aspect of this company. There isn't a job at this magazine that I haven't done myself or willing to do again. Our reputation as the nation's top magazine will maintain." Her eyes glared at the reporter. "Any more questions, Mr. Meadows?"

"That just about does it. It's a wrap."

The camera operator switched off his camera.

Houston smiled. "Thank you, Ms. Whitmore. This story should air tonight on the evening news."

"I'm looking forward to it. Enjoy the rest of your day."

He nodded, and then he and the camera operator left.

Angela rolled her eyes. "Francis, that was one of the worst interviews I have ever had. The guy is a complete jerk."

Monique approached Angela and Francis with a message in her hand. "I hate to tell you I told you so, but I told you so."

Angela rubbed the back of her neck. "How did you know?"

"I dated him in college. He was a jerk then. He hasn't changed."

"That's not important."

Monique handed her a message. Angela glanced at it. "Great, simply great. Another appointment canceled."

Francis smiled. "Look at the bright side, that gives you an opportunity to vet other potential clients."

"I suppose you're right."

Behind her, a platform on the outside of the window dropped down with the man in the Blue Bayou cleaning uniform whom Angela collided into on her way to work. He smiled and waved at everyone. He grabbed his squeegee and began to clean the windows.

Several of the female journalists stood as they stared googled-eyed at the window washer.

Angela's brows furrowed. "What is everyone staring at?"

Monique grinned and pointed toward the window washer. "Him."

Angela turned around; her eyes widened. "You've got to be kidding."

Francis swallowed and sighed. "I love the way he washes windows."

Monique nodded. "He can wash my windows anytime."

"I agree with you, Monique." Francis waved at the window washer again. "I wish he could come right through that window and get closer to me. I want to smell him."

One of the ropes that held the platform loosened, dropping the platform a couple of inches.

Monique's heart raced. "Oh, my God!"

Everyone in the room now focused on the window washer. The ropes which held the platform loosened again, jolting the window washer.

"He's going to die. We have to save him." Monique's eyes widened with fear.

Angela's clenched her jaw.

The window washer knocked on the window and yelled, but they couldn't hear him. He tapped on the window again as the platform swayed. "Open the window! Let me in. Please help me. Help." Only his mouth moved as the glass prevented anyone from hearing him.

Angela took a deep breath. "He's asking for our help. We have to get him inside before that thingamajig drops. Somebody, call for help." She tried to open the window, but it didn't budge.

Monique frantically dialed nine, one, one.

Francis bolted to the far side of the room toward the fire safety alarm system. She pulled it. The fire alarm sounded.

Angela threw her hands up into the air. "Why in the hell did you do that? He's not on fire. We have to get him in here before he falls. She continued to try to open the window as the window washer's face turned panic-stricken.

Richard Hastings, an overweight African American male journalist, grabbed a trash can and then ran toward the window. "Move out of my way. Step back; we have to break the window." He hurled the trash can in missile style formation toward the window. The trash can clang into it but bounced back, knocking the journalist backward, hitting his head on the corner of a desk.

Monique bolted toward Richard. "That's not what I had in mind for men falling at my feet."

Angela took control. "All right people, Plan B." She raised the left side of her skirt exposing a black lacy garter belt, thigh-high black stocking, and a leather holster with a semi-automatic gun and quickly retrieved it.

A bead of sweat formed across Francis' upper lip. "So, are you going to shoot him?"

Angela aimed her weapon toward the glass pane.

The platform dropped another couple of inches as the window washer's eyes widened. He put his hands in the air waving no and almost falls.

The platform jolted a couple more inches downward. It jerked and swayed more, almost sending the window washer off of it. He tousled but grasped the railing.

Angela waved her hands frantically for the window washer to slide to the left. "Move, I'm going to shoot the glass."

The window washer obeyed her command as he grasped the platform and kneeled.

"You're going to kill him." Monique put her hand over her eyes. "I can't watch."

Outside on Canal street, a crowd gathered as they gazed at the platform, which dangled and swayed. People bolted from the building chaotically as if it were on fire as sirens blared.

Houston and his camera operator immediately acted by broadcasting a live remote in front of the building. "I'm Houston Meadows, and I'm live in front of Benson Towers on Canal Street. Moments ago, a window washer almost fell to his death. Stay with us here at KWNC as this story develops."

Several fire trucks pulled up and stopped in front of the sky scrapper. The firefighters exited their vehicles and bolted into the building.

A news helicopter flew over and maintained its position, and several local news trucks pull to the side of the sky scrapper.

Angela aimed her weapon. Bang! Bang! Bang! The glass cracked. Bang! Bang! The glass shattered.

Angela handed her gun to Francis as Richard, and several of the journalists pushed the rest of the glass away.

Richard hurled the trash can toward the window, making an escape path for the window washer.

Angela and Richard pulled the window washer into the office just in the nick of time; the entire platform fell as the people below scattered. Smash!

The window washer landed face down in extreme pain as a pool of blood puddled around his left leg.

Monique's hands trembled as she returned the gun to Angela. "I don't like guns. They kill people."

Eight firefighters and four police officers led by Sergeant Danielson bolted into the area. The Sergeant eyed the gun in Angela's hand. "Put down your weapon."

Angela stepped forward. "Officer."

"I said, put down your weapon, now!"

Angela dropped the gun. Bang! A bullet ricocheted throughout the area sending everyone to take cover. Monique fell to the floor and rolled as she learned once in high school during a shooting drill.

The police officer approached Angela with caution as several paramedics darted into the room.

Richard grabbed his chest. "I'm having a heart attack."

Monique, now under a desk, fainted, and the rest remained gobsmacked.

Two paramedics rushed toward Richard and immediately performed CPR. The others dashed toward the window washer as the police officer handcuffed Angela.

"You have the right to remain silent…"

"…But, officer, I shot the window. I didn't shoot to kill."

"Tell that to the judge lady."

The window washer opened his eyes. The room spun; his vision went in and out of focus. "Excuse me, officer. She saved my life. She's my guardian angel."

Francis, grinning, sauntered toward the officer. She flashed a smile and batted her lashes. "Now, officer, that man would be dead if Ms.

Whitford didn't shoot the window." She glanced at the officer's name tag on his uniform. "Now wouldn't he, Sergeant Danielson?"

"Even if that were true, she discharged a firearm illegally. I'll have to take her in."

Angela pursed her lips. "Francis, call my attorney." *This is the worst thing that could have happened during my first week flying solo.*

"I'm on it." Francis bolted to Angela's office.

Sergeant Danielson escorted Angela toward the door just as the debonair striking John Legions entered. "Ms. Whitford?" His golden-brown eyes bulged. He swept his fingers through his thick raven hair.

"This isn't what it looks like." *My dad is going to kill me.*

CHILDREN'S SCARY CAMPFIRE STORIES

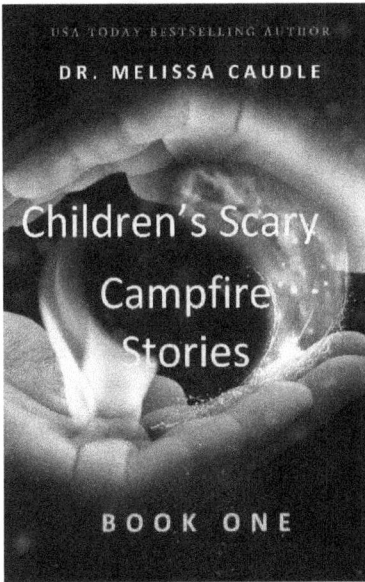

As summer approaches, it is time for families to prepare for their vacations. One of my favorite things is to go camping with all three of my daughters and their families. When the sun sets, we build a campfire that begs for campfire stories. The first thing my grandchildren do is ask for me to tell them a campfire story. Of course, they want me to make them up. Therefore, over the years I have created dozens of campfire stories. This book includes those stories and is appropriate for children of all ages. From the *Creek Dweller* to the *Crystal Magical Land*, these stories engage the imaginations. Don't let the word 'scary' stop you from purchasing this book as they are cute scary and not horror creepy appropriate for children of all ages.

AVAILABLE SUMMER 2021

CHILDREN'S SCARY CAMPFIRE STORIES EXCERPT

The Creek Dweller

[This story can be told with an accomplice secretly positioned out of view from the campfire ready to say their lines at the end of the tale.]

Once upon a time, there were seven children, six boys, and one girl, who lived in the middle of a bayou so big that it went on forever. Folks from the city tended to stay away because they were afraid of their cars becoming stuck and getting mud on their fancy clothes. Their neighbors stayed away too, but that was on account of tales that spread throughout on black magic. The legend said there was a spell that flowed through the roots of the giant cypress trees, which grew in the bayou. The children didn't mind a little mud, and they certainly didn't mind seeing a little magic, that is, if they ever found any.

One afternoon in August, when the swamp was so muggy that even the cicadas couldn't sing because their wings were too damp, the seven of them lay across the veranda panting and fanning themselves hoping for a whisper of a breeze to cool them off a bit.

"I'm hot," cried the littlest boy, whose name was Aryc.

"Me, too," answered Jax, who was two years older than his brother Aryc.

"I feel like I'm in a big oven," said Roger, who was several years older.

"I feel like I *am* the oven," said Eli, who was the same age as Roger.

"Stop talking, everybody. The hot air coming out of your mouths is just making me hotter!" complained Stamatis, the next boy who was five years older than Roger and Eli.

"You're talking, too," Jayden pointed out. He was the oldest, and not in the mood for all this complaining.

Stamatis was just about to argue back, but Blythe broke in, "Let's go play in the creek!" She was barely older than Aryc but clever for her age.

"Yes!" said Aryc and Jax together.

"No," said Roger. "It's too hot to go now."

"Yeah, but we'll cool down in the creek, and by the time we get back, it won't be so hot out," said Eli.

"Wait, guys," said Jayden, "You know Grandma's rule."

The other children nodded, and then chanted in unison: "Never go past the creek after dark!"

"Right," Jayden said. "It's already late. We'll have to go tomorrow."

"Come on," Stamatis argued. "We'll just go for an hour and come right back!"

"Just for an hour!" the other children chimed in.

Jayden frowned.

"Please?" begged Blythe.

Jayden shrugged. "All right, just for an hour, then right back here."

The children cheered. They all took just long enough to grab their towels and change into their swimming trunks and swimsuits, then marched down the veranda steps and headed straight across the yard going into the woods, picking their way over the roots of the old cypress trees and ducking under the hanging Spanish moss.

In ten minutes, they reached the wide creek which curved its way past their land. The water was green and slow, but Grandma had always warned them it was deceptively deep, and they must cross the bridge to play in the shallows on the other side.

Over the bridge they went, the littlest children holding onto the hands of the big kids so they could all safely cross the narrow plank bridge that straddled the shady creek.

When everyone reached the far bank, Jayden announced the rules. "No swimming, play where you can see the rocks on the bottom, and keep an eye on each other." Then he counted down. "Three, two, one... GO!"

They all jumped in with a mighty splash kicking up a big wave that rippled out across the green water.

The littlest ones plopped down in the water by the bank scooping up the muddy bottom with their hands and patting it onto their knees and shoulders, washing it off, and then doing it all over again. The older boys started a water fight, hooting and hollering as they chased each other up and down the creek, slapping and kicking the cool water at each other.

Jayden lowered himself into the creek and drifted out to the edge of the shallows with only his head and shoulders above water to keep a watchful eye on the younger children. He checked his waterproof watch now and then, but mostly he floated in the quiet water.

Blythe amused herself by building a mud castle on the bank. The youngest boys gathered near the bridge filling each other's sandals with moss. The older boys participated in a cannonball contest to see who could jump off a log and make the biggest splash.

Suddenly, Aryc stood up. "Hey," he said. "Did you hear that?"

"I didn't hear nothing," answered Jax.

"I heard it," said Roger.

"Me, too," said Eli.

"It sounded like a little voice," said Stamatis.

"A weird, sad voice coming from that tree over there," said Jayden. He pushed himself through the water toward the great cypress tree growing from the bank.

"Shhh," said Blythe. "Listen."

They all got really quiet, and from a dark hollow under the tree's roots came a soft, high voice, sighing over and over. "Nobody wants to play with me... Nobody wants to play with me..."

"Who's there?" asked Blythe. She waded nearer to the tree, bending down to look toward the hole. "Who's in there?"

"Just me," came the voice.

"Who's you?" asked Jayden wading over to Blythe. He drew her back by the shoulder and stood between her and the tree. "Show yourself."

The voice sighed. "You won't want to play with me."

"Sure, we will," encouraged Stamatis.

"Just come out!" said Eli.

"Sure," said Roger. "Come out and play!"

"Come out! Come out!" Jax chanted.

"Come play! Come play!" Aryc chanted.

Soon all the children joined in. "Come out and play."

"Okay," said the voice, and the children held their breath as they heard the water sloshing around in the hollow under the tree.

Then an eye appeared in the dark space followed by a frog-like face, and a slippery brown body of a creature about a foot long, like an overgrown salamander, but with one giant eye in the middle of its head emerged. It waded outstanding on its hind legs. The creature waved shyly, looking back and forth between the children with its one eye.

Blythe gasped. "Hello, I'm Blythe. Who are you?"

The creature paused a bit. "Well, I live in the creek, so I'm the Creek Dweller!"

"The Creek Dweller?" they all repeated.

"That's me, but nobody wants to play with the Creek Dweller."

"Sure, we do," said Roger.

"What do you want to play?" asked Eli.

The Creek Dweller tilted his head at Eli. "Well, what's your favorite color?"

"Blue!" answered Eli.

The Creek Dweller's brown skin blurred, then changed into a bright shade of blue that seemed to glow in the late afternoon sun. The children all gasped, then clapped.

"What about you?" asked the Dweller, pointing at Roger.

"Green!" he exclaimed.

"Pshh!" said the Dweller. "That's easy!" Its skin swirled lime green.

Jax couldn't keep quiet. "Mine's orange!" he blurted.

The Dweller snapped his fingers and burst into a fiery orange color.

Aryc chimed in. "Do purple!"

The Dweller spun around and turned violet.

Stamatis stepped forward. "My favorite color is... plaid!" he announced.

The Creek Dweller looked up at him with its one eye. "A smarty-pants, huh? Oh, well." He clenched his eye shut and put his little hands to his head and concentrated for a minute. Then his skin began to crisscross with red and green lines and little yellow squares. He jumped into the air opening his eye and throwing his hands up as he landed with a splash.

Stamatis shook his head. "Yep, you're plaid, all right."

"Please, Mister Creek Dweller," interrupted Blythe. "My favorite color is pink."

"Certainly!" The Creek Dweller paused. "Wait!" He looked behind the children. "Someone else is coming."

They turned to see a long copperhead snake slithering across the riverbank toward them. Its scaly skin gleamed like metal in the setting sun.

Several of the smaller children screamed and rushed back, crowding around Jayden in the water. They knew a bite from a copperhead could mean death out in the bayou.

The Creek Dweller didn't seem to mind. It waded toward the shore up to the snake stopping right in front of it. "Do you want to play with me?"

The copperhead reared her broad head back hissing as its fangs bared.

"Watch out!" screamed Blythe.

The Creek Dweller rolled his one eye. "Don't you want to play?"

The copperhead struck, sinking her venomous fangs into the Creek Dweller's body, and then pulled back ready to strike again.

"Oh, well..." said the Creek Dweller. He clenched his eye shut and put his little hands to his head. His concentrated for a minute once again.

The snake began to twist as her mouth opened, thrust her tongue out without making no sound as her eyes started to bulge. Her eyes grew and grew, moving to the center of her head forming into one giant eyeball. Suddenly, the snake's fangs fell out, and then she started shedding her scales all over the beach revealing her slippery-brown skin beneath. Four bumps appeared stretching out into short arms and legs with little blunt fingers and toes. Finally, a high-pitched scream of pain rose into the darkening sky. The pathetic creature slithered away whimpering as she crept into the underbrush.

In the distance, the children heard the snake sob, "Nobody wants to play with me... Nobody wants to play with me..."

The Creek Dweller turned and faced the kids.

"Are you all right?" asked Blythe.

The Dweller brushed himself off. "Perfectly fine! Now, where were we?"

"We were playing the color game," said Blythe. "And it was my turn."

"Oh, right!" The Creek Dweller climbed onto the bridge and stood up tall. "Your favorite color is pink, isn't it?"

Blythe nodded and grinned with excitement.

"What kind of pink?" the Creek Dweller asked.

"Pink like a gumball?" Blythe's eyes widened.

The Creek Dweller curled itself into a tight little ball, turning a bright candy hot pink. "Or pink like a tongue?" He unwound itself and stuck out its long tongue at them, which turned the same hot pink. "Or pink like a pig?" He pushed his nose up and curled his tail into a spiral making oinking noises as it turned the color of ham.

The little kids all giggled, and Blythe clapped her hands as she jumped for joy.

The Creek Dweller bowed in the setting sun. "All right, you're next." He pointed at Jayden. "What's your favorite color?"

Jayden looked at his watch, stepping onto the bridge. "We have to leave. We were only supposed to stay an hour, and it's already getting late."

"Don't you want to play with me?" the Creek Dweller asked, moving in front of him.

Jayden froze. He answered very slowly. "Uh, yes, I do want to play with you, we all do! But, uh, well..." He hesitated, looking at the sun setting over the trees on the other side of the bridge. "I think you should have your turn first!"

"Oh, okay!" said the Creek Dweller. It turned to face everyone, and his one eye seemed to glow in the gathering darkness.

"My favorite color is... Red!" The Creek Dweller gradually turned red as he grew, taking the children in his arms. "You will always play with me."

The children didn't come home that evening or the next evening, or any other evening after that. The folks out on the bayou say that on a quiet night, if you hold your breath and listen, you can hear voices out among the cypress trees. Some of them are those of small children and high-pitched, while some are deeper and lower but all of them always said the same thing over and over.

[If you're telling this story with an accomplice, at this point, they should softly call the next line from the darkness, instead of you.]

"Nobody wants to play with us… Nobody wants to play with us…"

ABOUT THE AUTHOR

Dr. Melissa Caudle debuted her novels "Never Stop Running: A Novel on Reincarnation" and "A.D.AM. The Beginning of Life" as the #1 New Release on Amazon. She is best known for her book *The Keystroke Killer: Transcendence.* Her upcoming novels included *Secret Romances: A Forbidden Thirst for Love,* and *Reborn.* She also has several children's and educational books, including her new book *Scary Children's Campfire Stories.*

Her books have received five-starred reviews in Publishers Weekly, Booklist, Goodreads, and on Amazon. She also writes nonfiction guidebooks for screenwriters on how to create a one pager, write a logline, write a synopsis and more as well as a new series for authors. Her book "How to Launch and Market a Book: The Six Month Countdown," has received raved reviews and has become a staple for authors. She also has a series of adult coloring books called "Abstract Faces."

"Dr. Mel's Message," her blog, has more than 360,500 views/followers where she writes about myriad interests.

She enjoys the city life of New Orleans along with her husband Mike and their two sidekicks, a Tuxedo cat named Meow Mix and an American Gray Shorthair named Simone. She retired from a twenty-year career in education after writing a number one bestseller on crisis management which took her worldwide as a keynote speaker to educational conferences and entered the film industry where she experimented with various occupations: production assistant, director's assistant, travel coordinator, script supervisor, screenwriter, and director. However, she left that field in favor of pursuing her lifelong passion for writing. She does her best writing at her beach condo, on cruise ships, or in her sunny-patio-home office overlooking the paradise pool. For more information email her atdrmelcaudle@gmail.com or visit her website: www.drmelcaudle.com. To keep up with new releases or speaking events sign up for her blog at www.drmelmessage.com.

DR. MEL'S LINKS ALL IN ONE CONVENIENT SPOT

My Author Website
https://www.drmelcaudle.com

Dr. Mel's Message – My Blog
https://www.drmelmessage.com/

Subscribe to Dr. Mel's Message
https://mailchi.mp/49349c2474d8/drmelsmessage

***Never Stop Running* – Purchase Link**
https://amzn.to/2U47jYv

***The Keystroke Killer: Transcendence* - Purchase Link**
https://amzn.to/2ErQtgH

***A.D.A.M. – The Beginning of Life* -Purchase Link**
https://amzn.to/2H2ik9O

How to Launch and Market a Book: The Six Month Countdown
https://amzn.to/2UkNcoY

Subscribe to Absolute Author Blog
https://mailchi.mp/752e94da6e99/absoluteauthor

Social Media Sites

https://twitter.com/#! /DrMelcaudle
https://www.facebook.com/DrMelCaudle
https://www.facebook.com/The Keystroke Killer Fan Site
linkedin.com/in/dr-mel-caudle-650a4036

ADULT COLORING BOOKS

BY DR. MELISSA CAUDLE

One of my hobbies, other than writing, is drawing abstract faces in a Picasso kind of way. I put together my favorites in a series of Adult Coloring Books. You can buy them on Amazon, Barnes and Noble, and my website: www.drmelcaudle.com, and other online retailers. I also have my art for sale on my website and at The Family Tree Antiques & Treasures in Bay St. Louis, MS.

ABSTRACT FACES
Adult Coloring Book
Melissa Caudle

ABSTRACT FACES
Adult Coloring Book Vol 2
Melissa Caudle

ABSTRACT FACES
Adult Coloring Book Vol 3
Melissa Caudle

ABSTRACT FACES
Adult Coloring Book Vol 4
Melissa Caudle

ALIEN FACES
Adult Coloring Book
Melissa Caudle

Cubism Faces
Adult Coloring Book
Melissa Caudle

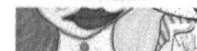

136

BOOKS ON FILM AND SCREENWRITING

WWW.DRMELCAUDLE.COM

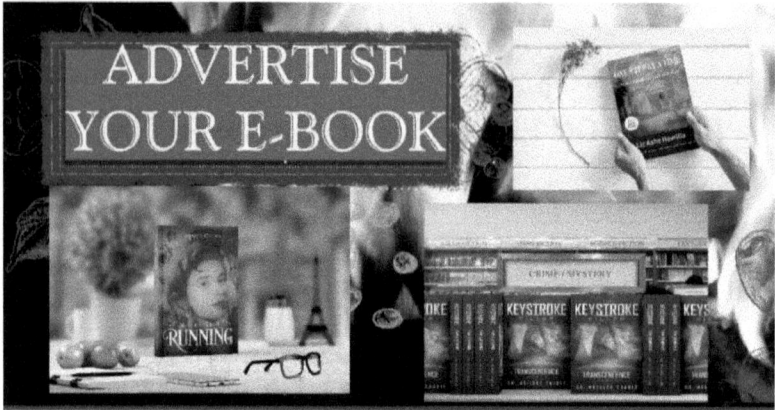

GET EXPOSURE FOR YOUR BOOK
BY ADVERTISING ON MY WEBSITE

Contact Dr. Melissa Caudle at drmelcaudle@gmail.com. As low as $5.

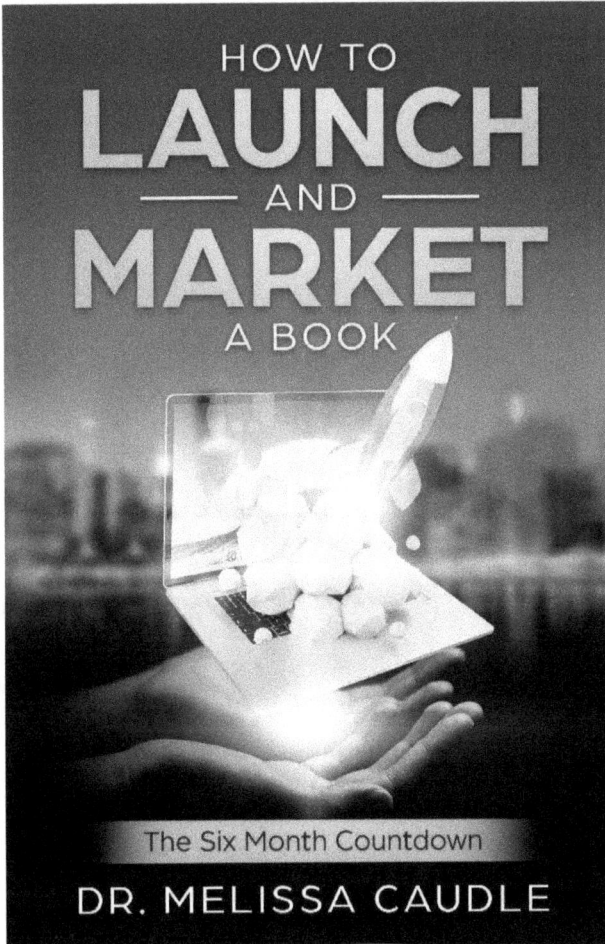

AVAILABLE ON AMAZON

Paperback, eBook, Audible

Narrated on Audible by Timothy Burke

BUY NOW

APPENDIX A

LIST OF ADJECTIVES TO DESCRIBE SUBJECTS FOR LOGLINES

- able
- adventurous
- ambitious
- blowhard
- bold
- bossy
- brave
- bright
- brutish
- busy
- calm
- carefree
- caring
- cheerful
- civilized
- clever
- clumsy
- compassionate
- conceited
- confused
- considerate
- cooperative
- courageous
- creative
- curious
- dainty
- daring
- dark
- demanding
- desiccated
- determined
- disagreeable
- dreamer
- drunk
- dull
- energetic
- excited
- expert
- fancy
- fearful
- ferocious
- fighter
- friendly
- fun-loving
- funny
- generous
- gentle
- gullible
- handsome
- happy
- hard-working
- helpful
- honest
- humble
- humorous
- imaginative
- immobile
- impulsive
- independent
- indolent
- intelligent
- inventive
- jovial
- joyful
- keen
- lazy
- leader
- lean
- licentious
- light
- light-hearted
- lovable
- loving
- loyal

141

- mannerly
- mean
- messy
- mischievous
- mottled
- neat
- obedient
- obese
- overweight
- patriotic
- perverse
- pitiful
- plain
- pleasing
- poor
- popular
- sad
- scrawny
- scruffy
- self-confident
- selfish
- serious
- simple-minded
- smart
- sterile
- strong
- stubborn
- studious
- successful
- tall
- thoughtful
- short
- pretty
- prim
- primitive
- proper
- proud
- quiet
- quarrelsome
- rawboned
- repugnant
- repulsive
- reserved
- resourceful
- respectful
- responsible
- rich
- rude
- shy
- simple
- thrilling
- timid
- tireless
- ugly
- uncoordinated
- unselfish
- unsuitable
- vacant
- violent
- vivacious

MY ADJECTIVE LIST GROWS

As your skill in writing loglines, add your favorite or new adjectives to describe characters in the list below.

_____	_____	_____
_____	_____	_____
_____	_____	_____
_____	_____	_____
_____	_____	_____
_____	_____	_____
_____	_____	_____
_____	_____	_____
_____	_____	_____
_____	_____	_____
_____	_____	_____
_____	_____	_____
_____	_____	_____

APPENDIX B

ACTION LOGLINE VERBS TO USE

- abandon
- abduct
- abolish
- abscond
- abuse
- accelerate
- accuse
- achieve
- acquire
- act
- adapt
- add
- address
- adjust
- administer
- advance
- advise
- aim
- allocate
- analyze
- answer
- anticipate
- apprehend
- approach
- appropriate
- arbitrate
- arrange
- arrest
- ascertain
- assault
- assemble
- assess
- attack
- attain
- audit
- avert

- bang
- bar
- beat
- berate
- bite
- blast
- block
- blow
- brighten
- broke
- buck
- budget
- built
- bump
- bury
- bushwhack
- calculate
- catch
- charge
- chart
- chase
- check
- choke
- clap
- clash
- classify
- climb
- clip
- clutch
- coach
- collapse
- collar
- collect
- collide
- command
- commandeer

- communicate
- compile
- complete
- compose
- compute
- conduct
- conserve
- consolidate
- construct
- consult
- contract
- control
- coordinate
- counsel
- count
- cram
- crash
- crawl
- create
- creep
- cripple
- crouch
- cut
- dance
- dart
- dash
- deal
- decide
- deck
- deduct
- define
- delegate
- delineate
- deliver
- descend
- describe
- design
- detect
- determine

- develop
- devise
- diagnose
- dictate
- dig
- direct
- discard
- discover
- display
- dissect
- distribute
- ditch
- dive
- divert
- do
- dodge
- dominate
- dope
- douse
- draft
- drag
- drain
- dramatize
- drape
- draw
- dress
- drill
- drink
- drip
- drop
- drown
- drug
- dry
- duel
- dunk
- ease
- edge
- edit
- eject

- elevate
- elope
- elude
- emerge
- endure
- engage
- enjoin
- ensnare
- enter
- equip
- erupt
- escape
- establish
- estimate
- evacuate
- evade
- evaluate
- evict
- examine
- exert
- exhale
- exit
- expand
- expedite
- expel
- explode
- experiment
- explain
- expose
- extend
- extirpate
- extract
- extricate
- fade
- fake
- fall
- falter
- fan

- fast
- fear
- feed
- feel
- fend
- fight
- file
- fill
- finance
- find
- finger
- fix
- flag
- flap
- flash
- flatten
- flaunt
- flay
- flee
- flick
- flinch
- fling
- flip
- flit
- float
- flog
- flounder
- flout
- flush
- fly
- fondle
- force
- formulate
- fornicate
- found
- fumble
- furnish
- gain

- gallop
- gather
- generate
- gesture
- get
- give
- gnaw
- gossip
- gouge
- grab
- grapple
- grasp
- greet
- grind
- grip
- gripe
- grope
- grow
- growl
- grunt
- guide
- gyrate
- head
- help
- hesitate
- hide
- hijack
- hit
- inflict
- influence
- inform
- inject
- injure
- insert
- inspect
- inspire
- install
- instigate
- institute

- hitch
- hobble
- hoist
- hold
- hover
- hug
- hurl
- hurtle
- hypothesize
- hack
- hail
- hammer
- handle
- hang
- harass
- haul
- identify
- ignore
- illustrate
- imitate
- implement
- improve
- improvise
- inch
- increase
- indict
- induce
- induct
- interchange
- interpret
- interview
- invade
- invent
- inventory
- investigate
- isolate
- jab
- jam
- jar

- jeer
- jerk
- jimmy
- jingle
- jolt
- judge
- jump
- keel
- kibitz
- kick
- kidnap
- kill
- kneel
- knife
- lash
- launch
- lead
- lean
- leap
- learn
- lecture
- left
- level
- lick
- limp
- listen
- log
- lunge
- lurch
- maim
- maintain
- make
- manage
- mangle
- manipulate
- march
- mark
- massage

- maul
- measure
- meddle
- mediate
- meet
- mentor
- mimic
- mingle
- mobilize
- mock
- model
- molest
- monitor
- motivate
- mourn
- move
- mumble
- murder
- muster
- mutilate
- nab
- nag
- nail
- needle
- negotiate
- nick
- nip
- observe
- obtain
- occupy
- offer
- officiate
- operate
- order
- organize
- oversee
- pack
- paddle

- page
- pander
- panic
- parachute
- parade
- paralyze
- park
- parry
- party
- pass
- pat
- patrol
- pause
- paw
- peel
- peep
- penetrate
- perceive
- perform
- persuade
- photograph
- pick
- picket
- pile
- pilot
- pin
- pinch
- pirate
- pitch
- placate
- plan
- play
- plod
- plow
- plunge
- pocket
- poke
- polish
- pore
- pose
- pounce
- pout
- pray
- predict
- preen
- prepare
- prescribe
- present
- presented
- preside
- primp
- print
- process
- prod
- produce
- program
- project
- promote
- prompt
- proofread
- propel
- protect
- provide
- provoke
- pry
- publicize
- pull
- pummel
- pump
- punch
- purchase
- pursue
- push
- question
- quit
- race
- raid
- raise

- rally
- ram
- ransack
- rape
- rattle
- ravage
- rave
- read
- realize
- receive
- recline
- recommend
- reconcile
- reconnoiter
- record
- recoup
- recruit
- redeem
- reduce
- reel
- refer
- regain
- rejoin
- relate
- relax
- relent
- render
- repair
- repel
- report
- represent
- repulse
- research
- resign
- resist
- resolve
- respond
- restore

- retaliate
- retreat
- retrieve
- reveal
- review
- ride
- rip
- rise
- risk
- rob
- rock
- roll
- rub
- run
- rush
- sail
- salute
- sap
- save
- saw
- scale
- scamper
- scan
- scare
- scatter
- scavenge
- schedule
- scold
- scoop
- scoot
- score
- scour
- scout
- scrape
- scrawl
- scream
- screw
- scrub

- scruff
- scuffle
- sculpt
- scuttle
- seal
- search
- seduce
- seize
- select
- sell
- sense
- serve
- set
- sever
- sew
- shake
- shanghai
- shape
- sharpen
- shave
- shear
- shell
- shield
- shift
- shiver
- shock
- shoot
- shorten
- shout
- shove
- shovel
- show
- shun
- shut
- sidestep
- sigh
- signal
- sip
- sit

- size
- skid
- skim
- skip
- skirt
- slacken
- slam
- slap
- slash
- slay
- slide
- slug
- smack
- smear
- smell
- smuggle
- snap
- snare
- snarl
- snatch
- snicker
- sniff
- snitch
- snoop
- snub
- snuff
- snuggle
- soak
- sock
- soil
- solve
- spear
- spell
- spike
- spin
- splatters
- splice
- split
- spot

- spray
- spread
- spring
- sprint
- spurn
- spy
- squeak
- stack
- stagger
- stamp
- stand
- start
- startle
- steal
- steer
- step
- stick
- stiffen
- stifle
- stomp
- stop
- strangle
- strap
- strike
- strip
- stroke
- struck
- stub
- study
- stuff
- stumble
- stun
- subdue
- submerge
- submit
- suck
- summarize
- summon
- supervise
- supply
- support
- surrender
- survey
- suspend
- swagger
- swallow
- swap
- sway
- swear
- swerve
- swim
- swing
- swipe
- switch
- synthesize
- systematize
- tackle
- take
- tap
- target
- taste
- taunt
- teach
- tear
- tease
- telephone
- terrorize
- test
- thrash
- thread
- threaten
- throw
- tickle
- tie
- tilt
- tip

- toss
- touch
- tout
- track
- train
- transcribe
- transfer
- translate
- trap
- tread
- treat
- trip
- trot
- trounce
- try
- tuck
- tug
- tumble
- turn
- tutor
- twist
- type
- understand
- undertake
- undo
- undress
- unfold
- unify
- unite
- untangle
- unwind
- update
- usher
- utilize
- vacate
- vanish
- vanquish
- vault
- vent
- violate
- wade
- walk
- wander
- ward
- watch
- wave
- wedge
- weed
- weigh
- whack
- whip
- whirl
- whistle
- wield
- wiggle
- withdraw
- work
- wreck
- wrench
- wrestle
- write
- yank
- yell
- yelp
- yield
- zap
- zip

MY ACTION VERB LIST GROWS

As your skill in writing loglines develops, add your favorite or new actions verbs in the list below.

_____	_____	_____
_____	_____	_____
_____	_____	_____
_____	_____	_____
_____	_____	_____
_____	_____	_____
_____	_____	_____
_____	_____	_____
_____	_____	_____
_____	_____	_____
_____	_____	_____
_____	_____	_____
_____	_____	_____
_____	_____	_____
_____	_____	_____

APPENDIX C

CHARACTER TRAITS FOR LOGLINES

- able
- active
- adventurous
- affectionate
- afraid
- alert
- ambitious
- angry
- annoyed
- anxious
- apologetic
- arrogant
- attentive
- average
- bad
- blue
- bold
- bored
- bossy
- brainy
- brave
- bright
- brilliant
- busy
- calm
- careful
- careless
- cautious
- charming
- cheerful
- childish
- clever
- clumsy
- coarse
- concerned
- confident
- confused
- considerate
- cooperative
- courageous
- cowardly
- cross
- cruel
- curious
- dangerous
- daring
- dark
- decisive
- demanding
- dependable
- depressed
- determined
- discouraged
- dishonest
- disrespectful
- doubtful
- dull
- dutiful
- eager
- easygoing
- efficient
- embarrassed
- encouraging
- energetic
- evil
- excited
- expert
- fair
- faithful
- fearless

- fierce
- foolish
- fortunate
- foul
- fresh
- friendly
- frustrated
- funny
- gentle
- giving
- glamorous
- gloomy
- good
- graceful
- grateful
- greedy
- grouchy
- grumpy
- guilty
- happy
- harsh
- hateful
- healthy
- helpful
- honest
- hopeful
- hopeless
- humorous
- ignorant
- imaginative
- impatient
- impolite
- inconsiderate
- independent
- industrious
- innocent
- intelligent
- jealous

- kindly
- lazy
- leader
- lively
- lonely
- loving
- loyal
- lucky
- mature
- mean
- messy
- miserable
- mysterious
- naughty
- nervous
- nice
- noisy
- obedient
- obnoxious
- old
- peaceful
- picky
- pleasant
- polite
- poor
- popular
- positive
- precise
- proper
- proud
- quick
- quiet
- rational
- reliable
- religious
- responsible
- restless
- rich

- rough
- rowdy
- rude
- sad
- safe
- satisfied
- scared
- secretive
- selfish
- serious
- sharp
- short
- shy
- silly
- skillful
- sly
- smart
- sneaky
- sorry
- spoiled
- stingy
- strange
- strict
- stubborn

- sweet
- talented
- tall
- thankful
- thoughtful
- thoughtless
- tired
- tolerant
- touchy
- trusting
- trustworthy
- unfriendly
- unhappy
- upset
- useful
- warm
- weak
- wicked
- wise
- worried
- wrong
- young

MY CHARACTER TRAIT LIST GROWS

As your skill in writing loglines develops, add your favorite or new words to define character traits in the list below.

_____	_____	_____
_____	_____	_____
_____	_____	_____
_____	_____	_____
_____	_____	_____
_____	_____	_____
_____	_____	_____
_____	_____	_____
_____	_____	_____
_____	_____	_____
_____	_____	_____
_____	_____	_____

NOTES

NOTES

HOW TO WRITE A LOGLINE TO INCREASE SALES

NOTES

NOTES